I0036636

Published by Tektran Incorporated
Edmonds, Washington 98020-0665 U.S.A.

©2020 by the Author: Ronald L. Bussiere, B.S.E.E.

Printed in the United State of America
1st Edition

ISBN: 0-9661128-3-0

Disclaimer: Company logos on or near any product displayed in this book are the sole property of those companies. Products displayed herein have not been tested nor are they being endorsed in any way. They are featured only as an example. Any GAAP or Tax related information offered in this book may be dated and should be verified by a CPA or tax professional. Therefore, neither the author nor publisher is liable for any damages or injury that may result in the use of any information or products that may appear herein. Any supply chain source information appearing in this book is provided only to be helpful. As always the reader is responsible for validating each item or method employed in practice to ensure it fits their application.

* All product and company names highlighted (*) are trademarks or registered trademarks of their respective owners.

Author ...

This book was written by Ronald L. Bussiere, president of Tektran, Inc. now retired. Ron is an electrical engineer with formal education and experience in operations and accounting. He has over four decades of experience in product development and manufacturing. He was responsible for drafting his company's three part Quality Management System (QMS) manual to comply with ISO 13485, the particular standard related to ISO 9001 and FDA QSR regulations. Tektran started in business in 1991, and was active for 25 years as an outsource design firm engaged in turnkey product development services for major players in the Medtech market as well as for professionally funded startups. Prior to that Ron owned and operated a medical electronics manufacturing business for nearly 20 years that sold his patented products through a network of distributors in the domestic market and through import merchants internationally. Ron was also responsible for developing Tektran's DCR (Document Control Record) system and the relational database eform record sets used by Tektran including the relational database reports for management – first using FormFlow* and later Formdocs*. Both of these software packages are programmed using Visual Basic and FAB code, respectively. Some of that script is displayed in the Appendix of this book. In addition to this book, Ron has written books related to manufacturing operations, cost accounting for complex multiple build level assemblies, and dozens of papers as well as technical books used by universities throughout the world related to RF/high frequency electromedical devices.

Preface ...

Although, the title of this book is "Physical Assets Management", it will cover depreciation of tangible assets as well as amortization of intangible assets since both normally show up on a Depreciation & Amortization Detail Spreadsheet.

Typically, CPAs or accountants are very good at numbers and/or dealing with tax code matters, but not so good at planning operations, nor is it something they normally engage. When setting up a complete system for management of physical assets you will find only 10% is related to accounting and 90% is related to operations planning as well as attention to internal controls and building safeguards into the process.

The entire Asset Management process should be displayed in a flow chart, like the one in Appendix A. After a careful review of that flow chart you can see it involves everything from the point of asset requisition to the asset's disposition at its end of useful life. That process may also include more than one participant, each with their own assigned task. That involves collecting and recording data as records are routed from one participant to the other. Routing will typically require its own flow chart or map along with user restrictions related to controlled access and authorization levels programmed into those relational database records as well as locked portions with each electronic signature.

Any operations process that works well will include: (1), policies; (2), directives; and (3), data collection records as well as a means to communicate all three of those elements to all the participants in the process. In a manufacturing concern that usually involves compliance with at least general standards like ISO 9001 or in the case of Asset Management, ISO 55000 and its particular volumes regardless what type of entity. From an accounting standpoint if you're a private concern you'll need to refer to FASB. If you're a government entity you'll need to refer to GASB as well as other state regulations for budget and reporting requirements. Each state varies in that regard.

Also, you just can't depreciate tangible or amortize intangible assets as you wish. There are a number of IRS publications that dictate the method you must employ, using tables that classify various types of equipment as well as conventions you must use to calculate depreciation for the first year based on the date assets are placed into service. Those tables are referred to MACRS (Modified Accelerated Cost Recovery) tables. It's a form of DDB (Double Declining Balance) depreciation, but uses a multiplier each year until cost recovery for each asset class reaches the end of its allowable recovery period.

With the IRS required MACRS recovery, salvage value is set to zero, meaning when you sell the asset you will pay tax as ordinary income for any sale amount that exceeds the remaining book value. GAAP (Generally Accepted Accounting Practice) as dictated by FASB is different than the MACRS tables and therefore, companies will often maintain two sets of books and Depreciation and Amortization Detail Sheets: (1) to comply with IRS regulations; and (2), to comply with FASB "Matching Principles".

Bonus depreciation under IRS section 179 is a separate issue. To grow the economy, the President and Congress passed what is referred to as "CAPEX" or a Bonus Depreciation up to 100% retroactive to 09/27/17 and good through 2022, using a declining percentage each year until it expires. That may over ride typical depreciation schedules. To see if your capital equipment purchases qualify, check with your CPA. Of course, before this does any good, your company needs to be making a profit.

There is also what they call "Safe Harbor" rules with respect to limited amounts for either capitalizing or expensing assets. Basically, the IRS says if you have "applicable" (audited) statements you can expense items up to $5,000. However, most small companies do not have their statements audited each year and therefore were allowed to expense assets below $500, except recently the IRS has increased that amount to $2,500 for companies without "applicable" statements.

Physical Assets Management – *The process from requisition to end of use*

Know that how you approach depreciation or amortization is as much about business and tax strategy as it is about asset management. Again, for that you'll need to consult with your CPA or Tax Attorney. I do not advise you to set your own depreciation or amortization cost recovery schedules for either GAAP or IRS MACRS without first being reviewed by a tax professional.

We will also cover Internal Controls as they relate to Asset Management. There are four areas of accounting that can leave your business or government entity wide open for fraud or embezzlement if you fail to maintain proper internal controls:

- Vendor Creation & Maintenance
- AP Accounts & Payments
- Cash Receipts
- Payroll
- Asset Management

It is imperative you set up controls within your organization to protect it and your stakeholders from such loses. AND beware – a general audit will not protect you from this kind of loss. The lack of internal controls is rampant in both private and government entities. If you doubt this, go to your state auditor's website where they list fraud cases – in most cases it's related to the four areas above. By the time most municipalities discover fraud, it's too late, so they typically look to their bonding agents to recover their **losses**, but like any other insurance as their experience rate goes up, so does their insurance premiums – all paid for by the tax payers of course. Then, there's the issue of book value vs. replacement value and the cost of proper insurance coverage.

According to published stats 75% of those employed in the U.S. steal from their employers at least once, and 37% do it repetitively. The losses are in the hundreds of $billions each year and this will only get worse as the mores of society continue to deteriorate. For example, there was a time when drug testing was unheard of, today for most employers it is a standard prerequisite before hiring as well as a background check which includes in many cases a view into a candidate's LNI claims history.

So security is an issued that is covered extensively in this book. Employers would like to think their employees, once vetted and hired are good, hardworking, and caring people and most are. However, it only takes a few to make a negative impact on everyone else in the way of lost revenues. If you don't build safeguards into your facilities and your processes, you're a fool. That doesn't mean your place of work has to be an armed camp, but safeguards should be installed and quietly put in place.

Of course, if you're not tracking both your capitalized and expensed assets you may never know anything is missing until someone needs that asset to complete a task. Then you find yourself purchasing the same assets or tools over and over. Therefore, security becomes an important part of the process surrounding Asset Management, and not only tangible assets, but intangible assets such as IPR (Intellectual Property Rights). Unfortunately, data falls into this category, making installing defenses against viruses and/or ransomware more important than ever before. Building firewalls, storage redundancy, redundancy conventions, network layout, utilizing routing records, passwords, and installing updated anti-virus software is only part of this defense planning. Establishing protocols and employee practices are also critical as well as communicating those practices to employees.

Internal controls can help defend against embezzlement or fraud by bad actors within your company or organization, but a plan to protect against thief or damages must include threats from both inside and outside your company or organization. All of this is part of the process and will be covered in this book.

Regarding software, I guess the best way to explain why I prefer custom software over canned software can best be made by looking at the flow chart that displays the process in Appendix A.

Physical Assets Management – *The process from requisition to end of use*

You can start with canned software and then attempt to come up with a flow chart displaying the total spectrum approach to operations related to Asset Management, but it would be like trying to pound a square peg into a round hole. ERP software poses the same problem. Most organizations are simply not ready for it in the way of personnel or skill sets. There are a number of SQL software products that can be employed to exchange data between EDMS and ERP systems.

Normally, processes in any organization must be configured around the staff available as well as their skill sets, with the exception of a few new hires to fill the gaps. For that reason I'm a firm believer is the use of relational database eforms where you can do your own thing and configure data collection records to conform to actual process as well as add whatever data fields on records that are needed. Property Records and Asset Disposition Reports can easily be developed to fit your process and from those record sets, using ODBC compliant databases or Excel spreadsheets, you can export eform field data to reports for both capitalized items as well as expensed items. With Formdocs* you can also import data into records using *Autofill* by using keyed source data from ODBC spreadsheets or databases residing on your server. All records are serialized with a consecutive seed and ending number for any given fiscal period in accordance with GAAP. Tablets running on a Windows OS can be used to take an inventory of asset items by department or within your entire organization on a periodic basis.

Although, capitalized assets will show up on your Depreciation and Amortization Detail Sheets by property number as prepared by your CPA, with the Safe Harbor limit now at $2,500 you'll want to keep a listing of all expensed asset items as well, whether stationary or mobile. With this new limit, the value of expensed asset items can easily now make up the lion share of your overall assets. If you're a government entity GASB actually requires that assets up to $5,000 be expensed. So, expensed assets can really add up and if not tracked can be a waste of resources when constantly replaced. Government entities also have GIS (Geographical Information System) infrastructure related assets buried underground that must be mapped and tracked to project their cost of replacement. Another use for RFID.

Using a proper schema for asset identification is important. See chapter titled, "Property of" labels. Once the asset is placed into service a map grid should be drafted to indicate the location if stationary. This involves nothing more than dividing each floor within your facility into identifiable grids and to keep that map on file when tracking assets during routine audits. Those grid indicators should be included on your Property and Mobile Tracking Record and in Asset Listings to aid inventory audits.

In addition to the use of barcodes, they're doing some amazing things these days with RFID technology. When this technology is integrated with video surveillance at each entrance or exit within your facility it can keep you from becoming a crime statistic. It can facilitate or ease the burden of taking inventory as well. We'll cover the possibilities in greater detail in chapter (6) titled, "Tracking Methods".

If you have a fleet of vehicles, today you'd normally employ GPS services to protect those assets and monitor their location at all times, using a subscription service (i.e. Lojack, Omnistar, etc.). Depending on the purpose of those vehicles a logistics plan would be an integral part of their use. When dealing with Fleet Management, the term that describes the technologies employed is called, "Telematics".

Assets are either Stationary or Mobile. Mobile assets are often assigned to employees upon hiring, or from a tool crib where they can be dispensed and checked back in as well as monitored for any needed calibration, repair, or preventative maintenance. When that is not practical, locked drawers or cabinets are often employed. In fact, the management of mobile assets includes many aspects, like types of locks, and even state employment laws that you might not realize when you try to hold an employee accountable for loss. Refer to chapter (12) titled, "Security" and chapter (14) titled, "Dealing with Bad Actors".

Table of Contents

Chapter 1   The Planning Process

Chapter 2   Defining Assets

Chapter 3 Data Collection Records

Chapter 10   Internal Controls

Chapter 11   Securing Assets in Place & in Storage

Chapter 12   Security

Chapter 13   RFID / Video Surveillance/Analytics - Integration

Chapter 14   Dealing with Bad Actors

Chapter 15   Conclusion

List of Figures

Chapters 1- 15

Appendix   **Page**

Note: The sample records and reports listed above and displayed in the Appendices indicated are put up in Formdocs* or MS Excel*. We used our DYMO* Label Writer 450 and its software to generate the PM Label appearing in Appendix L. We used NCH Click Charts* Professional version 3.01 to draft the flow charts appearing in Appendix (A) & (B). We used MS Word* to draft our QMS manual. Other parts of this book were created using Corel Draw*.

The one thing you may want to keep in mind while viewing each of these records and reports is whether or not the Asset Management software or ERP software module(s) you are looking at or have in place include the data appearing on these forms. If not, you may want to limit its use to accounting only or managing period Depreciation & Amortization for GAAP or IRS MACRS and leave the process records and reports to a more customizable software product whether it's Formdocs* or one like it.

Acronyms

1D	**1 Dimension or Linear Barcode – (i.e. Code 39 or Code 128 Symbology)**
2D	**2 Dimension Barcode – (i.e. QR Code or PDF417 Symbology)**
3D	**3 Dimension Barcode – (i.e. QR Code that uses colors for third dimension)**
AIIM	**Association of Intelligent Information Management**
ASC	**Accounting Standards Committee**
BLE	**Bluetooth Low Energy (an alternative RTLS technology)**
BPM	**Business Process Management**
CAPEX	**Bonus Depreciation as stimulated by the IRS** – enacted in 2018 to simulate the economy
CMMC	**Cybersecurity Maturity Model Certification**
Cloud	**Simply a Server in a Remote Location – A Safe Redundant Backup, normally secured by experts**
DB	**Declining Balance (Depreciation Method)**
DBMS	**Database Management Systems**
DCR	**Document Control Record (also used to mean Document Change Record)**
DMS	**Document Management System (also referred to as DCR)**
DDB	**Double Declining Balance** – also referred to as 200% DB
EAS	**Electronic Asset Surveillance**
ECM	**Enterprise Content Management**
EDMS	**Electronic Document Management System** - see detailed definition next page
EDRMS	**Electronic Document and Records Management System**
EPC	**Electronic Product Code**
ERM	**Enterprise Report Management**
ERP	**Enterprise Resource Planning** - see detailed definition next page
EU	**European Union**
FASB	**Financial Accounting Standards Board**
FNC	**File Naming Convention**
FOH	**Factory Overhead – also referred to as indirect cost**
GAAP	**Generally Accepted Accounting Principles**
GASB	**Governmental Accounting Standards Board**
GL	**General Ledger**
GPS	**Global Positioning System**
HF	**High Frequency (13.56MHz) RFID Band**
HR	**Human Resources**
IIM	**Intelligent Information Management**
IP	**Internet Protocol – typically a type of surveillance video camera – wired as opposed to wireless**
IRR	**Intellectual Property Rights**
ISM	**Industrial Scientific & Medical Frequency Band (13.56Mhz) – as assigned by the FCC**
ITAR	**International Traffic in Arms Regulations**
LAN	**Local Area Network**
LF	**Low Frequency (125kHz – 134kHz)**
MACRS	**Modified Accelerated Cost Recovery System**
NAS	**Network Attached Storage**

Acronyms – Cont'd

NOX	A surveillance system that combines video and RFID technologies – as well as other sensors
ODBC	Open Database Connectivity
POC	Principal Officer(s) Certification
POE	Power over Ethernet – as opposed to a non-powered Ethernet cable
PRA	Public Records Act
RAID	Redundant Array of Independent Disks
RFID	Radio Frequency ID
RTLS	Real Time Locating System (employs RFID technology)
SAP*	Systems Application and Products – for data processing – also ERP software & trade name
SIG	Special Interest Group – a standards organization for BLE (Bluetooth Low Energy) Straight
SLN	Line (Depreciation Method)
SOX	Sarbanes-Oxley Act
SQL	Structured Query Language - see detailed definition below
SYD	Sum of the Year Digits (Depreciation Method)
UHF	Ultra-High-Frequency (normally covers a range of 860 to 960 MHz for RFID technology)
UOP	Units of Production (Depreciation Method)
UVR	Universal Video Recorder
UWB	Ultrawide Band (up to 10.46 GHz) – an alternative RTLS technology
VPN	Virtual Private Network
WCM	Web Content Management
WIFI	Wireless Fidclity conforming to IEEE 802.11X Standard - a wireless networking technology

DEFINITONS:

Impairment	A Decrease is Cost Basis – due to loss (i.e. fire, theft, misuse, etc.)
Safe Harbor	Meaning - to stay within the limitations as stimulated by the IRS
Telematics	Includes all technologies related to Fleet Management – monitoring asset location & logistics

EDMS - An **Electronic Document Management System (EDMS)** is a software system for organizing and storing different kinds of documents, also referred to as eForms.

ERP - **Enterprise Resource Planning (ERP)** is business process management software that allows an organization to use a system to integrate applications in order to manage a business and automate many back office functions related to technology, services, and human resources.

SQL - **Structured Query Language** is the standard language for communicating with relational database management systems. SQL statements are used to perform tasks such as update data on a database, or retrieve data from a database.

Chapter 1 – The Planning Process

1.0   Overview

Before any process can be properly implemented a plan is required. This plan should be modeled based on the industry you in and the prevailing compliance standards as well as your staffing level and the skill sets currently in place. You can scale the Asset Management System (AMS) process using your current staffing level or if warranted you can hire to fill any gaps you anticipate in the process. The Flow Chart illustrated in Appendix A, describing the process from beginning to end should apply to any type of business. You will need a three part Quality Management System Manual or Operations Plan that includes: (1), policies; (2), directives; and (3), at least the data collection records displayed in Appendix C through X. A Routing Chart illustrated in Appendix B displays the action and recording assignments for each participant in the Procurement Process – the front end of any AMS.

Of course, before you can assign any task to an employee, you first need to know they are familiar with the task and are trained to perform it. That typically requires some degree of formal training. We'll cover training at the end of this Chapter and you will note in Chapter (3) we list data collection records to facilitate training and certification. The actual templates to document your training program are displayed in Appendix W. Once designed, they can be used for new hires or replacements. The final steps in the planning and implementation process are to verify that the elements are functioning as required and those elements working together are validated to achieve the desired result. Once those steps are completed you will need to monitor and audit all elements and the entire process periodically to ensure efficacy and that all events are correctly documented.

1.1   Strategy – Cash Flow Considerations

You may have heard the old motto, "Cashflow is King". This applies to Asset Management as well. That said, your first goal should be to keep your operating costs variable as opposed to fixed. Once you purchase and begin using an asset it becomes an ongoing burden whether it is used in operations above the contribution line on your Profit & Lost statement or used below as a burden to Administration, Marketing, or Research & Development. Therefore, you would be wise to perform a cost/benefit or 'make or buy" analysis before adding a fixed overhead burden. If the asset introduces a level of automation that impacts labor then that brings with it a whole new set of considerations. Refer to section (1.7).

At what capacity will you be using the asset? Can you load it so it's running at near capacity? When computing the total cost, including maintenance - would it be cheaper to outsource or sub-contract for whatever part that asset will produce? Don't forget the cost of floor space, utilities as well as the labor to operate and maintain the asset or the burden of any related warranty service contract. If you're a job shop and produce parts for other companies, that might be an easier decision as opposed to a company that only uses the asset for its own captive production. Vertical integration in industry was once popular but with all the job shops and service industries available today, unless you can justify the fixed burden it makes little since.

This axiom also applies to buying "real property" as opposed to leasing space; however, "real property" has its own set of GAAP edicts and IRS tax regulations governing depreciation and is a separate area of study. For that reason it will not be covered in this book. If you do build, it usually involves securing what they call "take-out" or long term financing and then with that in hand, arranging for a shorter term construction loan. Take-out lenders are normally large financial conglomerates, such as insurance or investment companies. A dog-and-pony show with architectural drawings and scale models is common practice along with all the zoning and building permits in hand - continuant before closing. Hence, Commitment Letters are often used.

Factory Overhead (FOH) burden is typically computed by adding all the burden or indirect cost related to manufacturing and dividing by the total cost of direct labor in a given period, normally each month. Which means - direct labor cost per unit of production is multiplied by that resultant coefficient or rate. For example, 2.5 times each DL hour. In order to remain competitive the goal is to keep that burden rate as low as possible. Consider the impact on your P&L and the rate by which the IRS will allow you to recover the cost as well as the period depreciation expense that will be distributed to your factory or GNA operating burden – above the contribution line or below it, respectively. Consider how that period expense will be shared with each department – manufacturing, administration, marketing, or R&D and how it may impact that departmental budget. Remember, usually costs above the contribution line on the P&L, are driven by sales. Expenses below are budgeted based on projected cashflow. However, capitalized fixed assets are a fixed burden. That said, no doubt every company needs a list of essential assets to operate.

Based on tax laws, the month you purchase the asset will play an important role in determining what first year convention you are allowed to employ – affecting first year cost recovery. Refer to Chapter (8).

The rule of thumb in corporate finance is – never use short term capital to purchase long term assets. Always finance equipment or long term assets with long term debt to leverage growth. The asset item itself can be used as collateral (at least in part) when securing the loan. Again, "Cashflow is King". Use short term capital and short term debt to finance your production and operating needs only. Of course, long term debt can only be secured when your level of profitability can service that debt. Some organizations Fund Depreciation which means to set up a liability reserve to pay for assets at least in part when they need replacement. This might work best for a non-profit organization or when securing a bank loan is difficult.

Later in Chapter (8) we'll discuss the difference and purpose between GAAP ("Book Method") depreciation and depreciation under IRS regulations or cost recovery under MACRS tables. Refer to IRS Publication 946. Fact is, you may have more flexibility selecting depreciation methods under GAAP and the prevailing edicts published by FASB or GASB than you would for tax purposes.

About the only flexibility the IRS provides a business, is to opt for the highest Safe Harbor limit with respect to the amount used to determine whether an asset item is expensed or capitalized. For most companies, that do not generate audited or "Applicable" financial statements each year, that limit used to be $500. It was recently increased to $2,500. The purpose was to reduce the number of assets a company had to carry on its Depreciation & Amortization Detail Sheets. You don't have to use $2,500 but it is normally recommend you take the tax deduction if possible. Larger companies or entities with Applicable financial statements are allowed to expense assets up to $5,000. Keep in mind you still need to list expensed assets and track therm. The higher limits for many businesses mean that list may end up being more in dollars at cost than capitalized assets, especially if your business does not maintain heavy equipment or vehicles.

Under GAAP you may wish to weigh carefully, the depreciation method used, depending on how it impacts your bottom line profits. In other words, your company's relationship with the IRS is different than that of the SEC (if you're a public firm) equity markets and/or Banks. Typically, the IRS wants to slow your firm's cost recovery in order to levy taxes from your company. IRS section 179 "Bonus" depreciation, commonly referred to as CAPEX was enacted for a limited period to prime a stagnant economy. AND from all indications it worked. In a way it puts conventional thinking regarding IRS MACRS tables on its ear; however, depending on your financial situation and projected goals, you may not wish to use it. In other words, you may want to confer with your CPA or tax attorney before using "Bonus" depreciation to access its impact and/or even applied. In other words, what's more important, given your situation – showing more depreciation expense or a higher book value?

GAAP method accounting is established to ensure a fair representation of your company's financial performance and position to protect those engaged in the equity and credit markets, by making sure everyone is playing by the same rules; hence, FASB and GASB edicts. Financials for the IRS falls under a separate set of rules. Yes, this requires two financial statements.

Also, if you're using an accelerated cost recovery method such as DDB (Double Declining Balance) depreciation the book value after depreciation will decrease faster than if you were to use SLN (Straight Line) depreciation.

Of course, when amortizing intangible assets the SLN method is used and the rate is based on the true "useful life" of the asset as dictated by GAAP or the IRS, whether that be a software, copyrights, product trademarks, patents, patent assignments, licensing agreements, or other intangible assets. Company trademarks are not amortized as they as renewable indefinitely – only product related trademarks.

Finally, after any allowable "Adjusted Cost Basis" due to an increase or loss ("Impairment") event, the positive difference between the sale price upon disposal and book value is considered gain and is taxed as ordinary income. Therefore, salvage value will determine the remaining book value upon disposal. Of course, there is nothing that says you have to dispose of an item immediately after its use and you can either donate it or sell. If you anticipate a slow period or downturn in business, you could wait to sell it then to realize the gain. Of course, one-time gains, if material, are required to be disclosed in notes to the financial statement.

1.2   Compliance Standards

If you're in the manufacturing business you should already be familiar with the general international standard for best practices or ISO 9001. Each specific industry sector may have its own particular standard, such as ISO 13485 for the medical device industry. Of course, for Physical Assets Management the benchmark international compliance standard is ISO 55000. GAAP edicts and IRS restrictions dealing with depreciation and amortization although part of the process, they have more to do with accounting methods as opposed to the process of managing and tracking assets, and are covered separately in Chapter (8) titled, " Methods of Depreciation & Amortization".

1.2.1   ISO 9001

This is the general international standard for best practices in the manufacturing industry. As mentioned, there are a number of related particular standards for specific industries that expand on the general standard. Subparts of ISO 9001 relate directly to Asset Management such as (7.1.3), (7.1.5), (7.1.5.1), and (7.1.5.2).

1.2.2   ISO 55000

Regardless what industry you're in ISO 55000 is the benchmark standard for Physical Assets Management. There are actually three parts or volumes:

> ISO 55000:2014 Asset management – Overview, principles and terminology
> ISO 55001:2014 Asset management – Management Systems – Requirements
> ISO 55002:2018 Guidelines for the application of ISO 55001

> Note: Standards are continuously updated as are tax regulations. Always check for updates.

1.3   Process Flow Chart

The process illustrated by the flow chart displayed in Appendix A should be universal regardless of the industry or business in which it is applied. If fully documented and audited each step as presented should represent best practices for Asset Management. As you draft the policies, directives, and data collection records as well as develop your training program we recommend you use ISO55002 as your guide.

1.3.1   Visualizing the Process

As you view the flow chart in Appendix A it is recommended that you visualize each event in the process. The process may vary slightly based on the size of your organization and the technology you employ. For example, if you use a legacy method to label and track assets, using barcode "Property-of" labels only or barcoded labels in combination with an RFID/RTLS (Real Time Locating System), the process at least at the point where tracking begins will change. Also, the first method tracks assets periodically and the second employs technology capable of tracking assets in real time. As covered in Chapter (6) and (11) tracking typically includes both stationary and mobile assets. Tracking mobile assets often requires a Tool Crib from which assets are consigned and returned and those events are both controlled and documented. As covered in Chapter (12) and (13), RFID technology can be integrated with video surveillance to track and protect assets from loss or by theft. RTLS technology can be used for asset protection at all perimeter exits for security or for the purposes of logistics within a business to monitor and improve operations.

When an asset reaches the end of its useful life an Asset Disposition Report is typically prepared which records its transfer to a Property Reserve or quarantined area where the asset is either sold or disposed of by way of a donation. This can be done in-house or via an auction house, under contract. Either way its sale or donation will need to be recorded for book and tax purposes. If sold a Bill of Sale is required.

1.3.2   Identifying Process Participants

The participants you use to build out your Asset Management System will vary depending on your company's size and the nature of your business. As discussed in the proceeding section, the process will also vary based on the technology you employ to label and track the assets. For example, this new digital age we are in, is giving way to a host of new job titles and skills never heard of before. Schools can hardly keep up, and in many cases training is left to professional associations, vendors, or the employer. Here's a list of considerations as you select participants for the various tasks illustrated in Appendix A:

(1) Where it would take place in your business
(2) What additional resources will be required to perform the tasks
(3) Who within your organization may be best suited to perform that task
(4) The distributed workload in man hours as you identify participants
(5) What new hires may be needed and with what skills
(6) How you might pair the participant who performs the task and the one who approves their work
(7) The training required – refer to sections (1.3.3) and (1.3.4)

1.3.3   Incorporating Procedures to Ensure Communication

The Formdocs* eforms program includes a number of features to facilitate routing. These features are activated as soon as you add two or more Filler licenses. With each eform used in the Asset Management process you can add a *Routing Slip* which can be set to alert and track all participants as the eform is completed and send along to the next participant in its path to completion. You can also build automated features into each eform so with one *Action Button* on the eform it will send everyone in the process an alert that an asset item has been received at the unloading dock and is pending inspection by the appropriate department head or Facility Manager, for example. Other alerts can also be programmed into these eforms. Directives should also be included to ensure communication wherever required. After validating the process a cover page should be drafted where each participant signs off on their assigned responsibilities.

1.4   Routing Flow Chart – introducing internal controls

Designing a routing chart for the process participants is much more than just drafting a step by step connection between each participant or displaying the handing off records to be completed. Refer to Appendix B to view a typical routing flow chart and a list of participants. This is only an example.

At this point, I need to stop and say that here is where most canned Asset Management software programs fail with respect to internal controls.   Software is required that incorporates best practices for internal controls.   To do that it must include programming features for: (1), controlled access; (2) ensure authorization; (3), provide for segregation of duties; and (4), be able to lock tasked data fields with e-signatures. Formdocs* incorporates all these features and more and you don't need to be a software programmer to configure e-form records the way you want them. The software features mentioned below are illustrated in greater detail in Chapter (10) titled, "Internal Controls".

1.4.1   Segregation of Duties

One of the most important features of GAAP based Internal Controls is *Segregation of Duties*. In other words, for anyone who is tasked to handle money or assets within your organization, the best way to avoid fraud is to require two separate signatures: one for the employee executing the task; and one for the Supervisor or Department Head approving the task performed.

1.4.2   Controlled Access

Formdocs* not only control access to the form itself, it includes various levels of rights such as read only or the right to fill key data fields related to each participants assigned tasks. Within the routing features you can incorporate a wide variety of limitations for each participant.

1.4.3   Authorization - Setting Limitations for Each Participant

Within the routing features you can incorporate a wide variety of limitations for each participant.

1.4.4   Locking Data Fields by Signature

Formdocs* incorporates a number of features that in effect lock Data as last approved. In other words the person who performed the data entry task can lock their work and after the Supervisor or Department Head adds their signature to the record – all data is locked. This enforces *Segregation of Duties*. It even allows you to employ a third party date and time stamp validation service like Digi-Stamp*.

Disclaimer: Neither I, the author or the publisher have a vested interest in Formdocs*. Prior to using Formdocs* I used FormFlow* for my data collection record sets. FormFlow* was developed for the DoD by Delrina* in Canada and later acquired by Symantec* It was eventually acquired by Adobe Systems* and life ended in 2004. FormFlow* used Visual Basic script and Formdocs* employs what they call FAB script. You can copy most script you'll require to automate these eforms from the sample templates you get with the program. It takes a little while to come up to speed, but once you do the ability to customize is almost without limits. You can also autofill data using ODBC databases to eliminate the need to fill repetitive data and add an Export button to generate spreadsheet reports for management. Formdocs* offers an SDK kit that extends its scripting and Com features.

1.5   Flow Designations

In addition to using ISO 5807 standards for flow chart symbols or shapes, you'll note in both Appendix A & B (numbers) are used over each step in the process. You'll want to use these designators when drafting both your Process and Routing directives as well as to identify specific data collection records employed at each step in the process. You should also use these designators when preparing a list of participants and their assigned tasks. They should also be referenced under each participant's signature on any *Sign-Off* sheet. Also, since a picture says a thousand words, you'll want to both reference and include a copy of all flow charts with your directives. Since people come and go in any organization I advise using job titles in the directives as opposed to Employee Names or Numbers, with the exception of *Sign-Off* sheets.

1.6   Quality Management System (QMS)

Whether you refer to it as a Quality Management Systems Manual or Operations Manual, when drafted in compliance with the applicable standards it will include: (1) policies; (2), directives; and (3), data collection to records. These are normally put up in a three volume set. Each page in the policy and directive volume sets will include a heading with two signatures: the CEO or General Manager and whoever is responsible for Quality Control. Some organizations employ a Chief Compliance Officer who's responsible for drafting operating manuals and training personnel as well as auditing personnel performance and process efficacy. This includes internal audits to support accounting to ensure financials are accurate. An Ops Manual for Asset Management can be a separate set of documents and only reference a QMS Manual.

1.6.1   Policies

Typically, policies included in any QMS or Operations Manual will follow either, FASB or GASB as well as the international recognized standard for Asset Management such as ISO 55000 and its parts (i.e. ISO 55001, and ISO 55002). These are all standards. IRS MACRS tables are laws. FASB and GASB are edicts for acceptance in equity and credit markets. The easiest way to draft policies is to use the same section and subpart designation that appears in the applicable compliance standard or edict. Policies normally are not written in order of the process flow, where directives are.

1.6.2   Directives

Directives should always reference both the applicable policy sections and subparts as well as data collection records that apply to each specific task within the process. Directives should be drafted to reflect your company's available resources with the exception of any new hires you will require to implement the process, but also demonstrate the ISO standard and/or FASB or GASB edicts are being followed. Tradeoffs should be to do this at the least expense to your company, government entity, agency, or organization while at the same time respect the workload assigned to each participant.

1.6.3   Data Collection – GAAP based records including management reports

As mentioned in section 1.4.4 the relational database eform templates you see in the Appendix of this book were put up using Formdocs*. It is an extremely powerful program with a host of features to speed your company's data collection tasks. It's relatively inexpensive to start and you can add filler licenses as your company grows. A fully functional free trial Designer and Filler module are available on their website at: www.formdocs.com for 15 days, minus the Routing features which require two or more filler licenses to for that feature to be operable. Eforms are referred to as Electronic Document Management Systems (EDMS).

When this book was published, the price for the Designer and Filler module was about $270 and each additional Filler license cost $130. The program has a HELP section that includes examples of various features to automate records, like *Action Buttons, Boolean Calculations, Autofill*, and the ability to *Export* data from batch record sets to ODBC compliant database or Excel spreadsheet-referred to as Electronic Report Management (ERM). Look to Appendix Q for that FAB script. Using Autofill you can also Import data. For example, if you have previously filled out a Property Record with data like make, model, serial number, and cost if that information exist on a periodic spreadsheet report, you can pluck that data and Autofill those data fields on an Asset Disposition Report when documenting the asset's end of life without the need to enter repetitive data.

The routing features within Formdocs* are quite extensive. As mentioned earlier the programmed routing customized limitations and security features built into the program allow you to design your data collection record to ensure primary internal controls are part of your Asset Management System (AMS).

The data collection records related to Asset Management, are listed in Chapter (3) along with the specific purpose of each one in the process.

1.7   Taking Corrective Action

It's usually harder to make changes to an Asset Management System in place and operating. Often the biggest problem is employee resistance to change and the fear of job loss. If you plan on keeping everyone on board and only tweaking current task assignments to improve efficiencies or introduce GAAP based internal controls, your first order of business might be to ensure affected employees the changes planned do not mean pink slips or pay cuts. Let them know it may require some retraining in order to acclimatize everyone to revised task assignments, but the goal is to keep everyone on and perhaps divide up the work by hiring some new employees where gaps currently exist. It may be good, up front to let the employees concerned know where those gaps exist. Let them also know upon completion of that training they will be issued certifications they have put in their resume file - something of value.

You may want to keep an eye on employees who protest change too loudly or leave before the changes are put in place. You may want to review the accounts they worked on going back a few years just in case. If nothing nefarious is discovered, you can focus on the positive steps going forward. Introducing GAAP based controls into your company's operations has as much to do with IT as it does with the accounting process, so you will need to bring your IT manager into the effort at the outset.

Drafting a plan for corrective action will require a careful study of the following:
- Space Requirements – facilities may need to be re-configured to accommodate new task participants
- Technologies – review software and devices most suited for your records and tracking needs
- Work Measurement – review man-hour data to ensure the workload is spread evenly over participants
- A written plan detailing the new routing processes and task assignments should be drafted
- Include the added cost of your plan, review and submit it for approval if necessary

Before you begin making changes, keep key employees in place to handle daily operating functions, and only pull a few offline for retraining at a time. As you implement the plan for corrective action make sure IT verifies the functionality of all GAAP recordsets and reports and as an integral part of the validation process you should meet at key intervals along the way with participants to get their feedback. Carefully pilot run any new methods, while keeping the old system going in tandem until the validation process is complete.

1.8   Procurement

Most reported cases of fraud are perpetrated within the procurement process – this is the front end of any Asset Management System. The methods used to defraud are too numerous to list, but in most cases are due to the lack of GAAP based internal controls. This includes not building into the AMS: (1), segregation of duties; (2), adequate access controls (i.e. passwords and absence of locked data); (3) not including proper authorizations or limitations for each tasker in the routing process; (4), the lack of GAAP record keeping; and (5) the lack of routine internal audits. Another way to reduce fraud is to give everyone in the process **Read-Only** access to various records, like the Purchase Orders or Property Records. This, in effect ensures a second-set of eyes on transactions. The procurement process is illustrated by the flow chart in Appendix B.

Critical policies and operational procedures include: (1), establishing a method to maintain and periodically audit a system for approved vendors and periodically reviewing those used; (2), forcing "Ship To" addresses by IT control other than by inserting them manually (see sample PO in Appendix F); and (3), the lack of review and approval by supervisors of "Payable To" addresses or vendor bank account routing numbers. These controls reduce losses not only related to assets, but also material/supply items. The use of a Daily Receiving Log is critical to maintaining control of purchases and deliveries. In the manufacturing industry it can help identify materials responsible for recalls and narrow recall lots, potentially saving $millions. See Appendix G. See how the pack lists with asset items are identified.

Other cases of fraud involve unauthorized transfer or theft of assets due to a lack of tagging, recording both capitalized and expensed assets, and then not routinely tracking them and/or not maintaining a system for asset disposition for assets that go missing or reach their end of life sooner than expected due to the lack of flags for routine preventative maintenance. Tracking involves a schema for identifying a location and a special system for tracking "theft sensitive" mobile assets. Theft increases with the lack of locked and controlled storage cabinets or tool cribs which can also be used to monitor the need for preventative maintenance, replacement, and/or calibration as assets are consigned and returned. A process for the proper care of assets becomes a tool for savings as well as a flag used for planning departmental budgets.

Of course an AMS is a total spectrum approach and requires a method to record the disposal of assets whether that be via donation, auction, or sales directly out of a property reserve. This is also when you are required to report gain or loss based on Net of Depreciation or remaining Book values.

1.9   Personnel Training

Regardless how well designed and documented the process is, personnel training requires constant revisions to reflect changes in operations due to growth or downsizing. Also, if you expect to build any *Sustainability* into the process as employees or participants come and go, documenting the entire training program for each task and ensuring that all participants understand the purpose of their task in the scheme of things is critical. This includes the curriculum, testing method, certification, and auditing process.

1.9.1   Identifying Qualifications

You will need to verify if an employee has the necessary prerequisite skill sets to even comprehend the training required as well as review the qualifications of any new hires needed to fill each position. The smaller you are the more difficult this can be. One way to do this is to prepare entry test to determine skill sets before wasting your time. Attitude has much to do with it too. Some employees may balk at the idea of accepting more duties without the offer of some added pay inducement, so there is that consideration too.

Don't forget to document prerequisite qualifications or certifications to ease the process of filling vacant positions as employees come and go. The best place to do that is in a Job Description HR can keep on file. As your company or organization grows you may need to update these documents prior to each use.

1.9.2   Developing Training & Certification Programs

Before developing training programs to fill the positions in the Asset Management process, you will first need to complete a set of policies, directives, and the data collection records detailing the entire Asset Management process and each participant's part in it. After validating the process itself it may be necessary to make changes or additions to the training curriculum for each process participant. I've included two eforms for documenting the course curriculums and training certifications, displayed in Appendix W.

The training program should reflect the specific tasks assigned to each participant. Cross training is advisable in case one or more participants are either absent or leave before you can find a replacement. It's normally recommended that you test participants with a written test to ensure they comprehend the task at hand and their part in the process. In addition a pilot run under close supervision should be conducted and the results should also be recorded. Normally, certifications are kept in HR with the employee file. Training curriculums, testing, and certifications should all be documented so you only need to pull it out when needed. Maintaining records like this will also help you stay compliant with operating standards.

1.9.3   Auditing Training Programs for Efficacy

Just like you'd build a working prototype to prove a concept and then build a protocol quantity of preproduction models to validate build documents before transferring them to production, you should do the same when auditing your training programs. One way to do that is record the seed record number and revisit employee performance after some protocol quantity of records are completed. This would be a good time to gather all the participants together in one room, if possible, where problems can discussed and revisions are made. Don't forget to Rev Code each revision in process documents and data collection records. All your company records or eform templates should be managed using a DCR (Document Control Record) system as covered in Chapter (3).

1.10 Verification & Validation

First, the verification and Validation process itself should be documented, reviewed by management, and signed off as ready for use. This is the best way to visualize what parts are required and how to proceed.

Verification has more to do with the individual tasks and data collection records. In this case you'll want to check whether each data collection record has the necessary data to properly record the event.

You then want to make sure the features programmed into each eform template are functioning as intended. Data field names are also key when exporting to spreadsheet reports with similar column names, so reports data is listed for each batch record set as needed for use by department heads or management. Generally speaking *Verification* is a test to determine if an item works by itself as it was intended by design.

Validation takes place once each individual task in the process is tested to see all the individual tasks and all individual records, are working together to provide you with the results required for the process as a whole and more importantly the process is in compliance with the required standards or other regulations you need to satisfy. The best method is to perform a pilot run and bring all participants and applicable department heads together to examine any possible missing elements or procedures. Once everyone is satisfied all is as it should be, participants, department heads, and executives should sign off on the *V&V* review. If the process needs improvement the process documentation and task records should be revised. Those changes should be recorded, using the DCR system covered in Chapter (3), section 3.1. Generally speaking *Validation* is a test to determine if an item works when combined with other parts in a process system.

1.11 Monitoring the Asset Management Process & Internal Audits

A periodic review of all batch record sets by fiscal period and their association management reports to confirm they are being property maintained will be required. That internal auditing process should be documented with a check list, the seed and ending record number for each record set in the process, and signed off by each task participants, department head, and the president or CEO. That audit checklist should be filed for future reference during an external audit.

Batch record sets and periodic reports stored on your LAN server and/or cloud account employing a documented storage and file naming convention. Those conventions should be part of the internal audit to ensure data is being properly archived and security measures are in place. See Chapter 3.

Enterprise Content Management (ECM) is a science all in its own. Your cloud service may have information to assist you with various file naming and storage conventions before you cast them in stone.

Chapter 2 – Defining Assets

2.0   Overview
Normally a fixed asset is either a building, equipment, furniture, a tool, an instrument, software, copyright, trademark, patent, or a written agreement that provides either an assignment granting rights, title, or interest, or a license to use that your business acquires to use for an extended period of time and is depreciated or amortized over its useful life to a business.

2.1   When Property is Purchased, Leased, Consigned, or Rented
First, before you can define property as a fixed asset to be depreciated or amortized on your financial statement you must determine whether it was purchased, leased, consigned, or rented. If you are entrusted to with someone else's property while under consignment or it's rented you should at least maintain a list of such property by make, model, and serial number as well as its market value. Consigned property is often provided by a customer and ISO 9001 refers to that as "Customer Supplied" property. Often the receipt you sign upon receiving such property it will state that it is being put in your company's care "under bailment" which means you are responsible for it until it is, either properly converted or returned. Neither, consigned or rented property is depreciated or amortized on your books and therefore does not show up on your Depreciation & Amortization Detail Sheets for GAAP or IRS purposes. If there is a fee associated with it while in your possession, that fee is treated as an expense.

Purchased Property is considered a fixed asset and is depreciated or amortized on your books starting with its cost basis. Its book value is based on its total allowed cost, minus accumulated depreciation or amortization.

Leased Property is normally displayed on your company's P&L and Balance Sheet as a fixed asset, but separately. Its cost is based on the total minimum lease payment during the full term of the lease. The residual value due at the end of the lease is considered its scrap value. Of course, this only applies if you have the right to purchase at the end of the term. If not, the payments are treated as an expense. However, in 2019 the tax laws changed for leased property and we recommend you consult with your CPA or accountant before recording these accounts or putting them on the books.

2.2   Capitalized or Expensed Assets
Whether an asset is either capitalized or expensed depends on it total allowable cost and what the IRS publishes and calls, "Safe Harbor' rules limits.

2.2.1   The Term Applicable Financial Statement
Safe Harbor trigger points that determine whether an asset is capitalized or expensed is first determined whether a company publishes *Applicable Financials* which simply means audited statements. Most small or medium size firms do not publish audited financials and therefore are treated differently.

2.2.2   Safe Harbor - Limitations
Those firms with *Applicable* or audited financials can expense assets can expense assets up to $5,000. Firms that do not generate audited financial statements used to be allowed to expense items up to $500. However, recently the IRS has increased that limit to $2,500. Where private companies have some flexibility to prepare their books using a lower limit than allowed can do so, based on restrictions stimulated by FASB or IRS regulations. However, government entities per GASB it is mandatory to expense all assets up to $5,000.

2.3   Tangible vs Intangible Assets

First, the term *Depreciation* is used when referring to cost recovery methods related to tangible assets and the term *Amortization* is used when referring to cost recovery methods related to intangible assets.

If capitalized, tangible assets such as furniture, computers, office equipment, lab equipment, instruments, tools, plant machinery, and vehicles are depreciated.

Intangible assets such as software, copyrights, product trademark, patents, and contract rights (i.e. patent assignments, private label or licensing agreements) are amortized over their use life if that useful life extends more than one year. Unlike tangible assets where there may be some options under GAAP regarding cost recovery or depreciation methods, intangible assets are normally amortized using the Straight Line (SLN) method. Commercially available software programs are normally amortized over three years. Refer to ISO/IEC 19770-1 titled, "Information technology-Software asset management".

When depreciating tangible assets for tax purposes under MACRS (Modified Accelerated Cost Recovery System) Tables the method employed for each group or asset classification is dictated by the IRS. Refer to the Appendices A & B in IRS Publication 946. There, the depreciation method, the recovery period in years, first year depreciation convention based on the date the asset was placed into service, and the recovery rate or period depreciation multiplier for each year are stimulated in a table.

2.4   Asset Classifications

As mentioned above, IRS Publication 946 includes MACRS Tables that divide assets into various classifications for depreciation and recovery period in years or life. Here's a list we used in our business:

Class
00.11   Office Equipment
00.12   Computer Equipment and related peripheral devices
00.13   Copiers, Typewriters, Label Printers, Adding Machine, and Calculators
35.0   Lab Equipment
35.0   Plant Equipment
34.01   Production Tooling
For software and other intangible assets refer to IRS section 179/197

Note: Some classifications can be used more than once to distribute period depreciation expenses to FOH (Factory Overhead) burden accounts or charged to departments under the Gross Margin or *Contribution Line* on a Profit & Loss statement such as Administration, Marketing, or R&D. They should appear broken out on your Depreciation & Amortization Detail Spreadsheets for GAAP and the IRS.

2.5   Stationary vs Mobile Assets

You will note the Property Record displayed in Appendix A of this book includes *Option Buttons* to indicate whether and asset is either *Stationary* or *Mobile*. By including this data it allows you to export to a separate list or spreadsheet report that contains only stationary or mobile assets to facilitate tracking or audits.

Obviously, stationary assets are items like desks, desktop computers, most types of office equipment, or non-mobile equipment or machinery on the plant floor.

If you look more closely at the Property Record displayed in Appendix K of this book you will see, using *Option Buttons*, it further categorizes mobile assets as either located and tracked : (1) a Tool Crib Asset; (2), a locked cabinet by department; (3), a locked drawer by workstation; or (4), consigned by HR to an employee.

Refer to section (3.16) for a sample *Tool Crib* control record. This serialized and date/time stamped record is used to record all consignments to an employee for a specific work/job order as well as record the return of those mobile assets. Locked cabinets in each department may be kept separately for various reasons.

For example, such a cabinet in a machine shop may contain very expensive hard tooling to be used on machines in that department. We recommend one key and a keypad type lock. Under the GAAP a Unit of Production method of depreciation would normally be calculated based on period production units and it life based on how many parts can be made with it before it becomes too warn for use. Tooling can be repaired and that repair cost may be treated as an increase to cost basis. If the tooling failed earlier than its original stated life, that may be treated as a decrease in cost basis – from the time of occurrence. If you're using IRS MACRS production tooling is classified as a (34.01) asset and depreciated accordingly. There may be exceptions, so consult first with your CPA.

In some cases, it makes no sense to issue tools or other smaller assets from a Tool Crib on a daily basis that are used by employees at their assigned workstations. For example, the long line of employees waiting for their tools in front of the Tool Crib daily and the wasted time before and after their shift would make little or no sense. On the other hand, entrusting keys to employees for workstation drawers containing such tools can be unmanageable. We recommend biometric locks on all workstation drawers or cabinets to serve two purposes: (1), monitor the abuse or wear of such assets; and (2) be in a better position to hold employees accountable for loss.

Holding employee's truly accountable for abuse or loss of assets is very difficult without competent proof. Federal and State laws vary in that regard. For further considerations regarding employee accountability refer to Chapter 14 titled, "Dealing with Bad Actors" and specifically section (14.2), (14.3), and (14.4).

If mobile assets like vehicles, cell phones, electronic tablets, or other mobile assets are consigned to employees a record of those consignments as well as a record of those returns should also be maintained.

Refer to the sample Property Record and PM Label displayed in Appendix (K) and (L) as well as the descriptions provided in section (3.2.17) and (3.2.18). These records are typically maintained in the employee's file in the HR department and will need to be referred to upon the employee's *Exit Interview*.

Fleet Management for any vehicles you either assign on a daily basis or for an extended period of time to an employee is typically monitored using *Telematics* which at the very least employs GPS tracking or other more advanced logistics. The mileage and condition should be recorded upon each return as should any *Preventative Maintenance* (PM) event.

If you park Fleet vehicles in a garage or lot, that area should be fenced and locked and monitored by motion activated video surveillance. This surveillance can be monitor in real time by you or an outside service. The Fleet Manager or whoever is in charge of these vehicles should make sure all vehicles are kept locked as well. If you have a number of vehicles this can be done with one master switch or with *Telematics* software.

The departure and return of Fleet vehicles can be monitored in real time via RFID or by integrating RFID with Video Surveillance at the gate and compared to a complete list of vehicles maintained, identified by number and/or how that identified vehicle may be detailed for specific use.

Chapter 3 – Data Collection Records

3.0   Overview

Most records listed in this chapter and in the appendix are relational database eForms, also referred to as Electronic Document Management Systems (EDMS) records. Data from these records sets are normally exported to Excel spreadsheets for management. Relational database eForms are customizable and follow Business Process Management (BPM) requirements for developing an Asset Management System. Regardless, any organization is going to have a number of other source programs and file extensions to manage as well. Refer to Chapter 4 for information regarding file naming and storage conventions.

GAAP Record Keeping Practices: Individual records in eForms record sets can be serialized with consecutive numbers per Figure 3.1 below to comply with GAAP record keeping practices, and put up in batch sets with a seed and ending record number for each fiscal period, where PDF or even Excel files cannot. Also, eForm records embedded in a batch record set are stored as one file with a (*.fdd) file extension where other records are saved as separate files. When starting a new batch record set for the next fiscal period, the seed record number starts with the next available consecutive number from the preceding batch. As you can see a prefix or suffix ide ntifier can be added to signify that a record set is processed by a specific employee or it could be used to specify a project or product model number; for example, when issuing a Change Order.

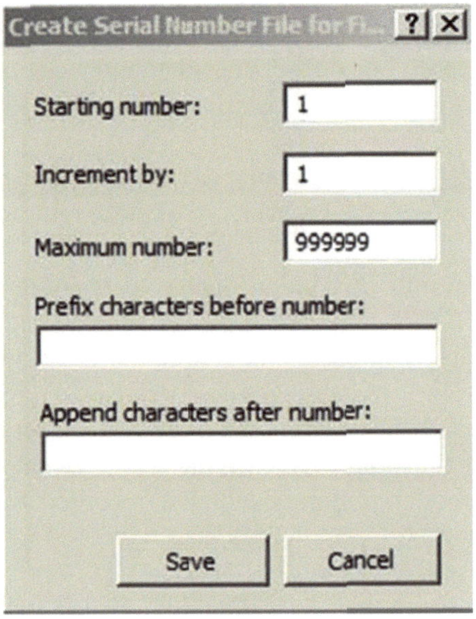

Figure 3.1

Internal vs External use considerations: Most operating records can be put up on eForms, some cannot.   For example, there currently is no free player program for eForms so if you need to send a fillable form to those outside your business a fillable PDF file is recommended. One example might be a web based fillable Application for Employm ent. On the other hand, most everyone has MS Office so sending out Excel or Word file is seldom a problem. However, for security reasons you may want to make sure it's protected. Some sources programs offer a free player and some do not. It is advisable to make a complete list of all source programs in use within you company or organization and include a written directive for external communications with those source program data files. As a courtesy, when sending a data file out you may wish to include a hyperlink to a free player for the file type.

3.1 DCR (Document Control Record) System

Data Collection is normally the third volume set in any Quality Management System (QMS) or Operations Manual along with policies and directives in volumes (1) & (2), respectively. Each eForm template or master template should have its own DCR number for identification and revision code, whether it's a record or report template. This third volume set should include a complete listing of every template in the volume set by revision code. Retired versions should be stored in archives.

If your company is engaged in manufacturing you should have a LIN (Line Item Numbering) scheme for raw material, components, and assemblies to track inventory and/or cost to facilitate multiple build levels or an exploded Bill of Materials (BOM). If you're a distributor you might employ a Stock Keeping Unit (SKU) identifier. You would be hard pressed to manage production or distribution without it. Same goes for your business records. In fact, there're a host of identification protocols for various records when running any business. Each one of those protocols should be documented in a directive.

Further, in order to comply with QMS standards we were required to not only maintain a list of control records by number that could be referenced with an *Action Button*, but also a record of revisions to each master template as well as the reason for each revision. Also, keep in mind these control records for operations were for repetitive processes.

To categorize eForm or other template files we grouped them by department, using the company org chart and designating a two digit code for each department on the chart. Refer to Appendix Y. The two digit department code was used as a prefix, then another two digit code for users at the 2nd line staff level performing the task and recording the process events, then a sequential number, and finally a revision code as follows:

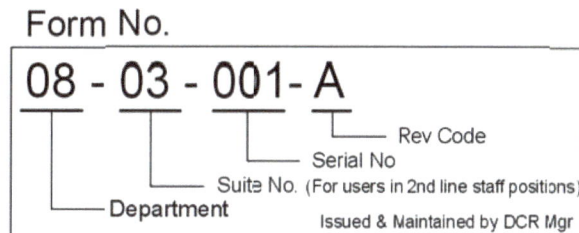

Figure 3.2

A schema for non-control records, are normally different. For example, product related literature, ads, price sheets, user guides or service manuals, etc. it may be more manageable if a different identifying protocol, perhaps using the model number as the prefix, followed by a code for the type of document, then the sequential number, and finally the revision code. Again, the schema and a list of identifiers should be maintained in a *Directive* that can be reference by the users engaged in related processes.

Although, the DCR Form No for an eForm template to record a Change Order should also be identified by department, each individual serialized record number using the template should also begin with the product model number (as the prefix), and then the consecutive ECO number. Refer to Figure 3.1

Therefore, in summary we have three different document identifiers: (1), the Form No; (2), the record number; and (3), the file name for the batch recordset or individual documents or reports. Folders and sub folders can also be used to sort these records. Some files may have to be stored manually after referring to a Directive. However, it is also possible to prevent placement errors by using script to force the location of at least MS Office and fillable PDF files. You can even force filenames for such files using script.

A host of schemas are covered in my book titled, "Line Numbering Schemes & Related Practices in Manufacturing" as well as their application in all areas of manufacturing, administration, accounting, marketing, and product development as well as contract management.

3.2   GAAP Records & Corresponding Flow/Routing Charts

Appendix A includes a Flow Chart of each step by step process in the Asset Management System. Each step is represented by a flow chart symbol and each symbol is numbered. That number will appear as a superscript after each form or step referenced in this chapter. Each section will include the Appendix where that sample form is displayed. Also remember, by granting viewing and/or data entry rights so process participants can perform their assigned task(s), there is no need for hard copies – go paperless! You can even disable printing to enforce that rule. Users can create desktop shortcut icons to speed access to record data.

3.2.1   Requisition [2]

This sample document is displayed in Appendix C. First, normally before a *Requisition* is prepared the user department identifies a need [1]. If the item(s) needed are material for production or supplies driven by sales, it is usually based on a *Shortage Report* as kits are filled, but should always require at least one other approval signature before sent on to purchasing. A *Requisition* should have enough detail with respect to type, and purpose to speed the approval or denial. Asset items are normally approved by a committee of at least the department head, and comptroller; or depending on the amount, the company or organization's operating executive [3]. Of course, all costs are reviewed before approvals are secured.

Directives are usually built into the process based on policies to determine the asset's total cost, and not just direct cost secured by an RFQ, but cost related to floor space requirements, additional utilities, installation, maintenance, warranty support, insurance, security, and personnel as well as debt service. Some assets will require a study to determine at what capacity it will be utilized and/or whether to carry the *Fixed Burden* or buy the part it helps make from an outside contractor, converting that projected fixed burden to a *Variable Cost*. Higher costs normally require approvals from those higher up the "food chain". Make no mistake. This is an important *Internal Control* document and the policies and directives set in place to control the process are to prevent fraud as well as to stay within departmental budgets and cash flow projections established in advance. The approval to purchase normally is not finalized until all costs are determined. [3]

3.2.2   Vendor Record [5]

This sample document is displayed in Appendix D. A Vendor Record serves a number of purposes. One is to gather a profile on your supply chain partners and to categorize various types of suppliers to assist purchasing in sourcing material, supplies, and asset items. It also serves as a record of Vendor Qualification which is a requirement for ISO 9001 QMS standards. Approval should always include two signatures, the Purchasing Agent who sourced or selected the vendor and the manager who approved the vendor.

3.2.3   RFQ – Request for Quotation [4]

This sample document is displayed in Appendix E. Normally, the make and model number of the proposed asset is known beforehand and its description is provided on the Requisition along with any combination accessories or supply items to operate it. If the asset requires additional service utilities be brought to it in the office, warehouse, or on the factory floor additional RFQs will need to be sent out to those contractors [4].

Any RFQ whether for an asset, combination accessories, supplies, or contract services should be sent from a list of preapproved vendors or contractors. Same goes for raw material, especially in cases where a blanket order or scheduled releases are under contract. Some vendors will also guarantee to meet the last price paid to help you maintain your cost of goods sold as well as discourage looking elsewhere for your needs.

The other consideration is when your company or organization is a member of a Group Purchasing Organization (GPO). If you are a municipality or government entity *Piggyback* purchases are often made with other nearby government entities or agencies to reduce cost. Normally GASB edicts and state regulations require as a participating *Partner* those in charge ensure by way of documentation that the host or lead entity followed all requirements with respect to bid laws and policies established by the *Partner* entity as well as other regulations. For example, does the state law or your government entity permit awards based on a *Point System* or the lowest bidder. The other question you might ask and get in writing is how will the asset warranty rights transfer to your entity as the participating partner. [5] [3]

If additional personnel are required, HR will need to be notified. If special training and/or skills are required, the vendor selling the asset may offer training. If not, other arrangements will need to be made. If the asset requires additional floor space the person in charge of facilities we need to be notified, etc.

3.2.4 Purchase Order [7]

This sample document is displayed in Appendix F. With viewing rights to the Requisition, RFQ, and final approval you should be able to prepare a Purchase Order (PO) [7]. A PO can also be employed as a directive to vendors. This is especially important in the Asset Management process where you'll need the *Make, Model, Serial Number*, and Net Cost listed separately for each asset on vendor invoice and pack lists. For example, some vendors without good discipline might refer to a PC desktop computer as a system and list one price and nothing else; whereas, the tower, screen, keyboard, and mouse have their own make, model, and serial number, and unit cost. You can't depreciate or expense an asset unless you can verify its cost. Note the option buttons on the Purchase Order eForm and how it causes an optional message to appear for asset items. Finally, the Comptroller should approve all PO commitments prior to release [6].

Using relational database eforms you can employ prefixes to batch recordsets, so for example if you have more than one Purchasing Agent, the transactions for each can be identified by their initials allowing everyone in the organization to see who prepared the PO. When that employee leaves the company or organization his or her batch recordset should be archived and a new batch should be created.

3.2.5 Daily Receiving Log [11]

This sample document is displayed in Appendix G. Here is where the receiving date, pack list number, and corresponding PO number as well as the carrier's tracking number is recorded. Note this eform also has a column to indicate if any capitalized or expensed assets were included in the shipment. If your organization has more than one receiving dock, this daily log should be maintained at each receiving portal. There are some sample recordsets we did not include in the Appendix, such as a Discrepancy Report used to process receipts that include wrong or damaged items. Typically, this record is sent to Purchasing for disposition.

Vendor Pack List: Of course, a vendor's pack list is a hardcopy document sent with the goods whether those goods are material, supplies, or equipment. Therefore, in order for that document to be part of your digital system you have to scan it, name that file based on your file naming convention for pack lists, and place that PDF file in a folder on your server, based on your Enterprise Content Management system. Normally, the vendor invoice number and pack list number are the same, so once the pack list is scanned and put into the system, the AP Clerk and the Manager can pull up a PDF of the reference pack list with a date/time stamp to verify the invoice list goods actually received and entered on the Daily Receiving Log. Refer to a copy of the sample AP Check Voucher in Appendix H.

The Receiving Manager is normally responsible to inspect the goods received against the vendor pack list and the purchase order to ensure that all items were received as they should be and to notify purchasing of any discrepancy.

There are at least three devices required in a properly equipped receiving dock in addition to a PC work station: (1), is a barcode and/or RFID reader; (2), a device for data/time stamping documents (like a vendor's pack list) with a system clock; and (3) a document scanner for creating a PDF of the date/time stamped pack list. Photos of typical a barcode scanner and RFID reader were included in section 6.2. Those also should be kept in a locked cabinet in the receiving area. Examples of a popular Date/Time Stamp machine and document scanner are displayed below in Figure 3.3 and 3.4:

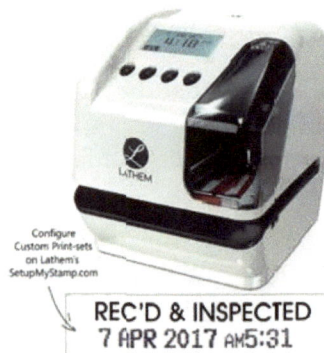

Figure 3.3 (*LT5000 Courtesy of Lathem*)

Figure 3.4 (*DocuMate 3125 Courtesy of Xerox*)

3.2.6   AP Check Voucher [10]

This sample document is displayed in Appendix H. Typically, before a check is approved for release it must be accompanied by a voucher that includes tracing information such as: a department requisition, the vendor's record number, the RFQ or Bid form number, the PO No, vendor pack list, vendor invoice, and the invoice amount. Here you can see the benefit of a relational database eform system that has the ability to include action buttons to quickly open each of these records as well as the Daily Receiving Log for verification. You can also see how it requires two signatures to ensure segregation of duties. The AP Clerk should have this eform completely filled out before handing it to the manager assigned to approve check releases. Creating phony vendors, phony invoices, and phony Payable-To addresses is common practice with embezzlers. Therefore, this voucher should always require a copy of the date/time stamped Pack List as proof the goods ordered were actually received and match the items on all other related documents.

3.2.7   AP Checklist - Payment Voucher [10]

This sample document is displayed in Appendix I. A *Payment Voucher* is a document normally used to secure approval from a *Comptroller* [6] to authorized payment for a batch of vendor invoices in an *Accounts Payable* (AP) cycle. As you can see from the flow chart in Appendix A, assets first must be inspected [11] for damage or other problems before AP [9] can include that vendor's invoice on the *Payment Voucher*. This is an Internal Control protocol that ensures what was shipped appears on the vendor's pack list as ordered. The employee tasked with the job of inspection should have viewing privileges to the PO, referenced on the Pack

List to compare quantity, make, model, and net cost. Then, if items received pass inspection the date stamped Pack List is delivered to AP. AP should not pay the corresponding invoice until the Pack List is stamped and signed by the Receiving Manager and Property Manager. The key to prevent fraud is to include *Segregation of Duties* throughout the Asset Management process and especially in the Procurement Process or front end of the AMS where most fraud takes place; which means, at least two signatures at each action point in the process- leaving no gaps in the double check process. A random periodic audit should be performed. Refer to section 3.2.24 or Appendix X.

3.2.8   Cost Basis Calculator [16]

This sample document is displayed in Appendix J. Although, a Cost Basis computation is listed on the Property Record, you will still need to break out the freight and sales tax if more than one asset item is listed on the vendor's invoice and pack list. This Excel template will do that so the process participant who is tasked with filling out the *Cost Basis Chart* on the Property Record can do so. The *Cost Basis* is the total costs paid for the asset that includes: the net cost, freight, sales tax, and even the cost associated with installation. A total Cost Basis Calculation is a requirement of FASB, GASB, and the IRS.

3.2.9   Property Record – including PM Event Record [13]

This sample document is displayed in Appendix K. The *Property Record* set is the most important record listing, categorizing, maintaining, and tracking assets – both depreciated and expensed assets. It is used to also track adjustments in each asset's cost basis, including additions and impairments to book value. Of course, if the impairment or loss is due to damage, fire, or thief then a *Disposition Report* should be filled out and accounting should be copied so they can reduce the book value accordingly. Refer to section 3.2.19

As you can see from the various data fields on the sample Property Record it is not only used to register the vendor, invoice number, description, make, model, serial number, cost basis, and date placed into service, but based on its cost basis and the policy you set for capitalization it is used to determine whether the asset is either depreciated or expensed. As mentioned earlier in section 2.2, a private company has some flexibility to set that dollar limit under the prevailing IRS safe harbor rule which is currently $2,500 where government entities are required to set the dollar limit per GASB at the maximum allowed. Currently that limit is $5,000. The sample template displayed in Appendix I is programmed to automatically fill the prefix in the asset identification number ("D" or "E") to indicate whether the asset is depreciated or expensed as soon as the total cost is calculated. If bonus depreciation is taken based on IRS section 179 it registers that as well.

In addition, it records the asset class, based on the standard classifications in IRS Publication 946 table and whether the asset is either stationary or mobile as well as the type of mobile asset. This data will determine how assets are stored, managed, and tracked.

It would be difficult to use or maintain an asset if information regarding combination accessories or related peripherals, disposable or recycled items, such as toner cartridges or refill items were not listed so those in charge of purchasing those items had one document they could refer to with reviewing privileges, so that information is included as well. The *Property Record* is the best place to do that.

Service techs or others in charge of *Preventative Maintenance* (PM) will often need access to asset information to assist them in their work also, so page (2) on the *Property Record* includes a table to record PM events. Keeping both sheets in one asset record satisfies that need. You can opt to show or hide cost basis information with the approval signature, giving viewing rights only to data required.

Some companies or organizations prefer to keep intangible assets on a separate *Amortization* register or listing. From there, those intangible assets are added to the Depreciation & Amortization Detail Sheet mentioned in the following section and used by your accounting department. We prefer to maintain that record on the same *Property Record* set so that record is automatically assigned a property number – in this case with the prefix "A" and a class indicating either software, copyright, trademark, patent or contract rights such as patent assignments, or licensing rights.

In addition to all the data that appears on this document, its main purpose is to assign a *Asset Number* in order to track and maintain the asset during its useful life and beyond. The *Disposition Report* mentioned in section 3.19 is autofilled in part by the data recorded and exported to a report from this *Property Record*. It would be very difficult to take an inventory in an orderly manner of either capitalized or expensed assets without the schema encoded into the *Asset Number*, appearing on the asset's *Property-of* label.

3.2.10 Preventative Maintenance Label [19]

This sample document is displayed in Appendix L. We have all seen how an auto mechanic who services our car maintains a record of each service event or oil change and at what mileage on a label pasted to the driver's side door jam. This label is pasted to machinery on the factory floor or equipment in an office, if it requires periodic maintenance so employees know when that asset item was last serviced. This template fits a standard DYMO label size and includes a place to record the service event date and the process control document used and its revision code. Refer to section 5.4 for information on various label materials.

3.2.11 Depreciation & Amortization Detail Sheets [16]

This sample document is displayed in Appendix M. As mentioned earlier, your accountant will normally keep two of these detail sheets: (1) for the tax purposes based on MACRS tables that appear in the IRS Publication 946; and (2) for GAAP based on FASB edicts. Government entities are required to follow rules set forth by GASB. This sample document is based on MACRS tables and the multipliers that appear on those IRS published tables by asset classification and the date the asset was placed into service. You will note those asset classifications follow the list that is displayed in section 2.4

3.2.12 Asset Reports [17]

This sample document is displayed in Appendix N. This report or one like it, can be generated for any asset class such as Capitalized, Expensed, Stationary, Mobile, or Type. This report is taken directly from the Property Recordset by using filters to export only those assets that you want to review. It is used to both prepare a management report and/or to track assets separately by class or in total. By sorting assets by class it can ease the burden of auditing inventory whether using legacy methods with grid maps and barcode labels or when employing an RFID RTLS (Real Time Locating System).

3.2.13 VBA/Marcos to automate file naming and reports [17]

Using Formdocs* FAB script to control EXPORT action can be written to export only that data that is needed to prepare the detail sheets referred to in section (3.2.11) and for tracking purposes. An example of this VBA coding is displayed in Appendix O. The report displayed in Appendix N is also taken directly from the Tracking Record displayed in Appendix P. However, a master database/spreadsheet can be created from the Property Records. As we mentioned earlier, government entities are required by GASB to expense all assets under $5,000. A private company can currently expense assets up to $2,500 according to the IRS, but by policy can set that limit lower as long as it's is written policy and remains consistent.

When classifying assets into groups you can facilitate the optimum method to track each group. As we mentioned mobile assets can be tracked from a tool crib or locked storage cabinets. HR should record consignments made to employees upon *Hiring* or returned as part of the *Exit Interview* process. This requires periodic inspection of locked cabinets or work station drawers. Access codes are normally issued to specific employees, whether for keypads or biometrics. Refer to Chapter (11) for additional information.

3.2.14   Asset Tracker [(17)]

This sample document is displayed in Appendix P. This sample record is put up in Formdocs* and runs on a Windows 10 tablet. We ran the one displayed on a NuVision* 8" tablet, MN TM800W610L. It can also run on a Panasonic Toughpad* MN FZ-E1. The NuVision* requires a Bluetooth barcode scanner, the Toughpad has the barcode scanner built-in. There are a number of enterprise tough tablets available in the $500-$600 price range. Some have NFC read capability. Using a pouch with a belt clip and a holster for a wireless barcode scanner you can pull up data on each asset. The asset can be located by using an image of floor plans with grid indicators stored on your tablet. Assets are more easily found using a Grid Map and a schema for the location code that appears in a data field on the Asset Tracker eform.

Using a spreadsheet report with any group of assets or all of them, you can IMPORT static data for any specific asset using the property number as the key. In other words, you only need to scan the barcode or RFID tag on each *Property-of* label to autofill the other data fields – data taken from the master database or spreadsheet. With this Asset Tracker you only need to record the CONDITION or COMMENT based on your audit and also flag management when that the asset requires service or calibration.

Finally, once the asset has been inspected you can confirm the audit event by clicking the button to date & time stamp the data field to the right. This eform will force you to SAVE prior to moving to the next record in the record set. The time stamp also discourages faking an inventory or not taking it seriously.

3.2.15   FAB Script for Asset Tracker [(17)]

This sample programming script is displayed in Appendix Q. The Formdocs* FAB Script displays how the named columns can be arranged in order on your spreadsheet report. It also forces the data into a temporary data file and uses the DCR Form No. as the filename. The script post instructions to a dialog box that pops up to instruct the user how to capture and transfer data to a permanent spreadsheet report file.

3.2.16   Tool Crib Record [(18)]

This sample document is displayed in Appendix R. This document is titled, "Tool Crib Receipt". As you can see this is a record of consignments to employees and return of each asset to a tool crib. The release date and time is recorded as well as the return date and time. To speed the process at the Tool Crib counter it is designed to record these events using the barcode on the employee's badge.

As we mentioned earlier a Tool Crib is normally a locked cage where specific mobile assets are stored and controlled. Upon return you can see there is a place to record the condition of the asset and instructions to notify management in charge of needed repairs, calibration, or refills.

Other mobile assets are stored in either locked department cabinets or work station drawers where specific supervisors or employees are responsible for their care. Refer to Chapter (14) for steps to prevent theft and information regarding federal and state employment laws when assets go missing.

3.2.17   HR – Consigned Assets Record [17]

This sample document is displayed in Appendix S, Part 1. Some mobile assets are consigned to employees upon hiring in addition to their badge ID. Since this record is filled out by HR it may make since for HR to maintain a secure cabinet in the HR department with those assets and manage their storage, release, and return from there. Also, as employees are hired, HR would be in the best position to alert management when additional assets or replacements are needed. Consignment of a vehicle may also be recorded on this document as well as a set of keys or it may be controlled by a *Fleet Manager*. Some private and public entities either consign a vehicle for continuous use while employed or it may be consigned daily from a motor pool. This document when completed is signed by the employee verifying they took possession of assets that are entrusted to their care.

3.2.18   HR – Returned Assets Receipt [17]

This sample document is displayed in Appendix S, Part 2. This is list of assets consigned to an employee and returned upon termination of employment or transfer. When the assets that were originally consigned to an employee are returned, a receipt is provided to the employee as acknowledgement and proof of return. As such, it is signed by the HR manager or the staffer in HR in charge of such assets. This document is normally a prerequisite to the employee's final paycheck or severance pay.

3.2.19   Asset Disposition Report [21]

This sample document is displayed in Appendix T.   During an asset's life it may fail, need repair, get damaged, reach its end of life, go missing, or transferred to a Property Reserve or quarantined area to be sold. To record these events and to alert management an *Asset Disposition Report* is prepared. This document is usually printed out and attached to the asset as it travels to its final disposition. It is also used to record a gain or loss, depending on the difference between book value and/or salvage value and the sale price –if sold. If donated you should be able to declare the salvage or scrap value. Using *Autofill* once you scan the *Property-of* barcode label other identifying data such as description, make, model, and serial number for the asset should appear. When using Formdocs* this information is taken from an up to date Excel spreadsheet report or ODBC compliant database of all the organizations capitalized or expensed assets. Various degrees of asset disposition will also show up in the Asset Report(s), displayed in Appendix N generated by the Asset Tracker, displayed in Appendix P.

3.2.20   Bill of Sale – A Property Reserve Record [24]

This sample document is displayed in Appendix U. Before an asset is either sold or donated, it is transferred to a Property Reserve or quarantined area for processing. As each asset is sold a Bill of Sale should be prepared to record the gain or loss and to provide the buyer with proof of purchase. Notice the disclaimer on the Bill of Sale stating that all sales are *"As Is and Final"*. It is also customary to remove all *Property of* labels as the asset is sold. In other words, a *Property of* label on an asset when in the hands of a new owner could invite liability claims, especially where large firms are concerned.

3.2.21   Batch Consignment Record – A Property Reserve Record [23]

This sample document is displayed in Appendix V. This is simply a list of assets that may be consigned to an auction house for sale. Note it can also be employed to set reserve amounts for each line item asset as well as identify them by general description, make, model, and serial number. It also requires that the auction house either return assets not sold or deliver an invoice with proof of payment for each asset sold which is normally the basis for their commissions, plus any other cost agreed to in advance.

3.2.22 HR – Course Curriculum

This sample document is displayed in Appendix W, Part 1. Personnel training is crucial if you want operations to run smoothly. The first order of business is to ensure whatever program that is put in place is *Sustainable*, especially as employees come and go or are transferred. The best way to do that is to catalog all video training programs and to number and identify them by course number as follows:

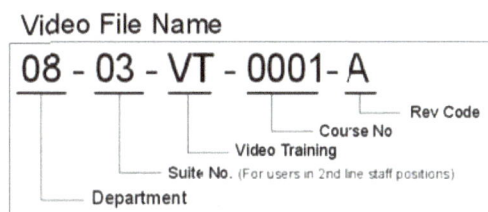

Video File Name

08 - 03 - VT - 0001- A

- Rev Code
- Course No
- Video Training
- Suite No. (For users in 2nd line staff positions)
- Department

Figure 3.5

If *YouTube* videos are used that log should include a list of any specific level of security. The three levels of security being: (1), public; (2), unpublished URL; and (3) password protected. We advised against using (1) for personnel training. A log should be maintained of all courses and training videos with: file name, revision code, description, URL, protection level, password (if sensitive), and viewing time.

As you can see the eForm titled, "Course Curriculum" is a multi-page template with a page to create a beginning and ending storyboard with video file names, titles, and other information – including credits and contact information for follow-up questions. Allowing employee(s) who help produce the video take credit for it which fosters pride and a desire to do quality work.

Note: Directly above the blank and fillable introductory and ending storyboards this document includes tips on producing and publishing YouTube videos for professional use as well as embedding them on web site pages.

Don't forget, *Communication* is key to the quality of any process; therefore, the compliance officer or supervisor administering the training and certification should make sure the employee knows how they fit into the grand scheme of things and why their assigned tasked are important. This includes signature and routing methods used to support the next employee in the *Routing Flow Chart*.

Videos or e-Media for marketing purposes should employ the same schema used for product related literature and sorted by product model number prefix.

3.2.23 HR – Certification of Course Completion

This sample document is displayed in Appendix W, Part 2. A "*Certificate of Course Completion*" is a record for internal use as well as to satisfy regulatory agencies. It is a proclamation that the subject employee has passed a training course and is capable of performing subject task(s) with minimal supervision. The test is usually administered by a *Compliance Officer* or the employee's *Supervisor*. It should be a written test and in most cases will include a pilot run where the employee's quality of work is inspected. It's recommended you conduct an inspection after the employee performs the task on their own during the normal course of business to make sure going forward he task(s) will be performed correctly.

It should be made clear to employees before training starts that this *Certificate* will be kept in their HR jacket and it is something of value they can hold onto and include with their resume if and when they might leave the company or point to during a *Performance Review*.

HR may consult with supervisors or the compliance officer to check the work performance. Attitude is a large part of any job performance and should be carefully monitored during training and the certification process. When an employee asks questions during training or certification that is normally a sign they're taking it seriously. Employee *Certification* is a requirement of ISO 9001 and FDA (GMP) QSR (Quality System Requirements). It is also part of any RA (Risk Assessment) process.

3.2.24 Internal Audit Report

This sample document is displayed in Appendix X, Part 1-3. An Internal Audit Report is employed to review the performance of each participant of the Asset Management System (AMS) as it appears in Appendix A, and mainly to ensure all recordsets in the process are being property maintained, named, and stored, whether on a LAN server or in a Cloud account AND based on a documented file naming and storage convention – all in accordance with GAAP based record keeping. Refer to Chapter 4. This report also ensures that the company's or organization's accounting records reflect the status of all assets and that all preventative maintenance is being performed and recorded as required. The job title for the employee who is tasked with this responsibility is often called a *Chief Compliance Officer* – a title that extends beyond just the AMS.

One of the most important functions of a CCO is to ensure all participants are properly trained to perform their assigned tasks and that includes developing training programs for each participant, to test, and certify each participant until they are performing their assigned tasks as required.

During the audit process, a review of how well each participant is communicating with each other and whether or not the company is communicating its requirements to each participant via access to video training courses or directives is important. Formdocs* allows for *Action Buttons* on the face of each eForm to pull up policies, directives, or even links to YouTube training videos. This feature is important for new hires or if the task assigned is not routinely performed.

The method used to communicate revisions to process participants is also important. This is normally done with an email notification as well as updated policies or directives. All links to directives should be current. This is usually the responsibility of the CCO and IT working together.

Reference Standards:
ISO 15489-1:2016 Information and Documentation Records Management - Concepts and Principles

ISO 27001-1:2017 Information technology –Security techniques - Information security management systems – Requirements

ISO 10012:2003 Measurement Management Systems - Requirements for measurement processes and measuring equipment.

ISO 17025:2005 General requirements for competence of testing and calibration laboratories

Chapter 4 – File Naming & Storage

4.0   Overview

In section 3.0 we covered *GAAP Record Keeping* principles which requires events to be recorded using consecutively numbered relational database records with a seed and ending record number for each fiscal period or batch recordset. In section 3.0 we also displayed the serial number generator dialog box inside of Formdocs* when setting up a batch recordset or *.fdd and *.fdn file.

Taking the time up-front to develop a strategic plan for *File Naming, Storage, and backup* is essential. A written Data Collection plan should **define** processes, strategies and tools that allow a business to effectively create, save, organize, store, archive, and retrieve data in order to deliver critical information to its management, employees, business stakeholders and customers. Archival methods should include a formal records retention policy based on your industry regulations and prevailing laws.

That system should include a plan for storage structure by folder and/or sub folders that reflect your operations. Refer to Appendix Y & Z for an example. Any software tools you employ to manage information should be included in your written *Directives* and update when revised. The plan should include *Directives* for file naming and storage conventions as well as the physical network or system *Architecture*, including LAN servers, Cloud accounts, NAS/RAID backup systems or other external backup devices – and how they are all connected. Refer to section 4.4 and Figure 4.2.

IT operations should include a documented plan for security management protocols covered in Chapter 12 and specifically section 12.7 as well as compliance standards. Personnel training programs should make sure those protocols are communicated to everyone using the network – whether desktop or mobile devices.

4.1   DFN (Data Field Naming) & Security Tips

Formdocs* requires an underscore between words for naming data fields as opposed to spaces or dashes. For example, a Field Name in Formdocs* may use a naming protocol such as: "Form_No" Field names should be short but relate to the labels above each data field on the template. Also, in order to export data from a relational database eForm to a spreadsheet report, the database field and Excel* column names should be the same. You can limit the exported data from key fields by specifying those fields in Visual Basic or FAB script when using Formdocs*. Refer to Appendix Q. Also, when copying and pasting data from data fields the field names in the source recordset and the columns in the target report will need to be the same.

Security Tip: When designing an eform template make sure you limit the number of characters in each text based data field to prevent hackers from entering your system and using an open data field (without character lengths) to load a virus.

4.2   FNC (File Naming Conventions)

First, when saving a relational database record or eForm you don't need to worry about writing over the eForm template. However, files put up in Excel* or fillable PDF it's easy to overwrite the master(s) if you're not careful. To prevent that, once the master is complete and ready for use, go to File Properties and make the file **Read Only** to force a *Save As* dialog box when you're ready to save your work product. That will force the *Save As* dialog box to open so you don't overwrite the master file – leaving the master file a protected template with its embedded functions, but a blank one with respect to data. These files are normally named by date as follows: 2019-FYE-(plus a short recognizable description) *. xlsx or *.pdf. Operations related control records should be named by date and their respective DCR No. as follows: 2019-08-01-001. Refer to ISO 8601:2019 Relational database eForm batch recordsets are place on your server or Cloud by your DCR or IT manager. A filename example for a Formdocs* file would be "08-01-001.fdd" Since a revision can be introduced in the middle of a recordset or batch using the save and memorize function, the revision code is left off the filename.

The work station user must refer to a *Directive* to ensure the file is stored in the right folder or sub folder on the server for future retrieval. In addition, it is necessary to maintain master templates of each as well as filled data reports in either *.xlsx and *.pdf file extensions or other file extensions. We recommend separate sub folders for masters and records. Other application files might use a project or model number as a prefix.

Also, although this may have more to do with storage than filenames, it is possible to write a simple macro or java script by inserting an *Action Button* in either Excel or a fillable PDF to force a *Save As* file into the correct folder on the server as well as name it, based on the data in a specific cells or data fields. This is a job for your DCR or IT Manager so they can police ECM. Refer to the bottom of section 4.3 for further details.

4.3   File Storage – ECM (Enterprise Content Management)

The AIIM (Association for Information and Image Management) is a global non-profit organization founded in 1943 for the microfilm industry, the leading authority for information management. There are many other professional IT related associations. Refer to a list of IT associations in section 4.4.

Information Management Science: The AIIM defines ECM as "*Neither a single technology nor a methodology nor a process. It is a dynamic combination of strategies, methods, and tools to capture, manage, store, preserve, and deliver information that supports organizational processes through its entire lifecycle*".

In March of 2017 AIIM retired the term ECM and replaced it with IIM (Intelligent Information Management). IIM is a more comprehensive term that encompasses technology advancements such as Cloud technology. IIM includes all of ECM. The distinction being IIM is not only includes the definition of enterprise content management above, but it also automates data. IIM is considered a system can be defined as a knowledge management system that organizes different kinds of business intelligence, not just content. File management software currently embraces both BI and AI technology and internet related commerce.

Compliance Standards: The compliance standard *ISO/TC 171/SC 2* was created back in 1994 for Document file formats, EDMS systems and authenticity of information. Currently there are a number of finalized standards. The one that references ECM directly is ISO 18829:2017 titled, "Document management -- Assessing ECM/EDRM implementations -- Trustworthiness". Another ECM recognized standard is ISO 22957:2018. In ISO 9001:2015 the benchmark standard for QMS (Quality Management Systems) refers to records management, subpart 7.1.6 refers to Organizational Knowledge.

Regulatory: In addition to compliance standards there are a number of regulatory issues that may apply to your business or government entity such as: SOX-Sarbanes Oxley; FDA & Data Retention Policies; PHI-Protected Health Information; PCI DSS-Payment Card Industry Data Security Standards; and others specific to your business. This may depend on the industry you're in or if you are private firm or government entity.

Connectivity: ODBC stands for (Open Database Connectivity) and is a standard application programming interface or (API) for accessing Database Management Systems. If you expect to pull data from an ODBC compliant database or an Excel spreadsheet for use in what Formdocs* calls Autofill, if you ever change the path location of the source database, make sure you change the path statement in the ODBC *.dsn file. To change the path to the source data file in Windows go to C:\Program Data(X86)\Common Files\ODBC\Data Sources\. Then look for the correct .dsn file and change the path inside this file (last line):

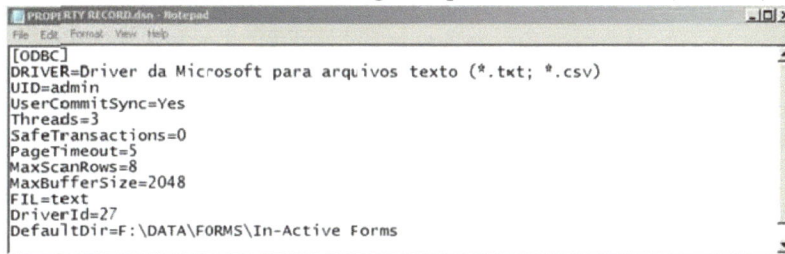

```
[ODBC]
DRIVER=Driver da Microsoft para arquivos texto (*.txt; *.csv)
UID=admin
UserCommitSync=Yes
Threads=3
SafeTransactions=0
PageTimeout=5
MaxScanRows=8
MaxBufferSize=2048
FIL=text
DriverId=27
DefaultDir=F:\DATA\FORMS\In-Active Forms
```

Figure 4.1

It's normally advisable to use a separate storage schema for operating control records, like the schema displayed in Appendix Y and a different schema for storage of all other data files. Some can be stored by project or product model number or other recognizable category. Adhoc files can be stored in alphabetically.

In a busy office you want to automate the process of saving and storing files. For control records and reports used for operations it can be confusing for employees to name and store records they don't work with on a daily basis. Therefore, it is well worth the time to write a **Macro** for Excel reports or **Java Script** for fillable PDF files that direct saved files to the correct sub-folder on your server and filename. Upon completion in Excel go to Developer and Marco Security and set it to "Disable All Marcos with Notification". The hyperlinks b elow will direct you to instructions to automate storage for both MS Excel and PDF reports:

https://docs.microsoft.com/en-us/office/troubleshoot/excel/save-file-to-network-drive

https://software-solutions-online.com/save-pdf-file-specific-user-defined-path-excel-vba/

https://acrobatusers.com/tutorials/how-save-pdf-acrobat-javascript

To generate and create Action Buttons inside of PDF files you will need Adobe Acrobat. Remember you will only need to include this on Excel and PDF masters that you use on a regular basis. The programming macros or script should direct the files to folders where the filled records and reports are kept. Appendix O includes VBA script to automatically name and store Excel files in a pre-designated folder.

Invoices & Pack Lists that come from your vendors or any other external documents should be converted to PDF and stored for auditing purposes. For those vendors who still mail hardcopies you'll need to scan these and file them under Vendor folders and then by date. Many vendors have moved to emailing PDF copies of invoices. You might consider placing a note on your PO instructing vendors to email PDFs and if they send hardcopies as well mark one "Duplicate". Of course, *Pack Lists* are hard copies sent with the goods.

4.4   Access & File Retrieval

Access is normally controlled by the employee charged with IT security as well as setting limits to what each user can do or not do with each file or even data entry by data field. When designing eForms or masters IT should lock specific data fields after e-signature approvals are saved. Excel master should not only be made *Read-Only*, but format, macro, scripts, and formulas embedded should be protected by passwords known only to those responsible in IT. Formdocs* offers three levels of security: (1) view only; (2) data entry; and (3) the right to change the eForm template itself as well as any features embedded in it. Those in IT are normally charged with the task of creating new batch recordsets as needed and policing all stored data.

Retrieval: Desktop shortcut folders and icons on each user's work station can be used to access relational database files on a LAN Server, based on their assigned tasks. This can be done with relational database eForms because you're adding new records and data to those serialized records in one batch recordset – all contained in one file. When using Formdocs* that includes the recordset file with an *.fdd extension and the key or *.fdn file extension to control the data in each data field on a record based on the record serial number. Shortcuts can also be used for Excel and fillable PDF masters as well. If Excel reports are filled using data export features built into Formdocs* or other relational database records, after the report is complete it can be named and saved to the designated folder either manually or automatically as explained in section 4.3

A practical approach to ECM is to employ a coded Org Chart, identifying each department with a prefix and a file storage map displaying a directory path or tree, accessible at each user's workstation as a reference tool, at least for the files that pertain to their tasks. Refer to Appendices X and Z.

4.5 Network System Architecture - LAN Servers, Cloud Storage, and Backup

Obviously, the level of complexity and sophistication of your Network System Diagram will depend on the size of your operations and your network goals. The network system diagram in Figure 4.2 addresses the typical connection LAN servers, Cloud Storage, and Backup as well as workstations:

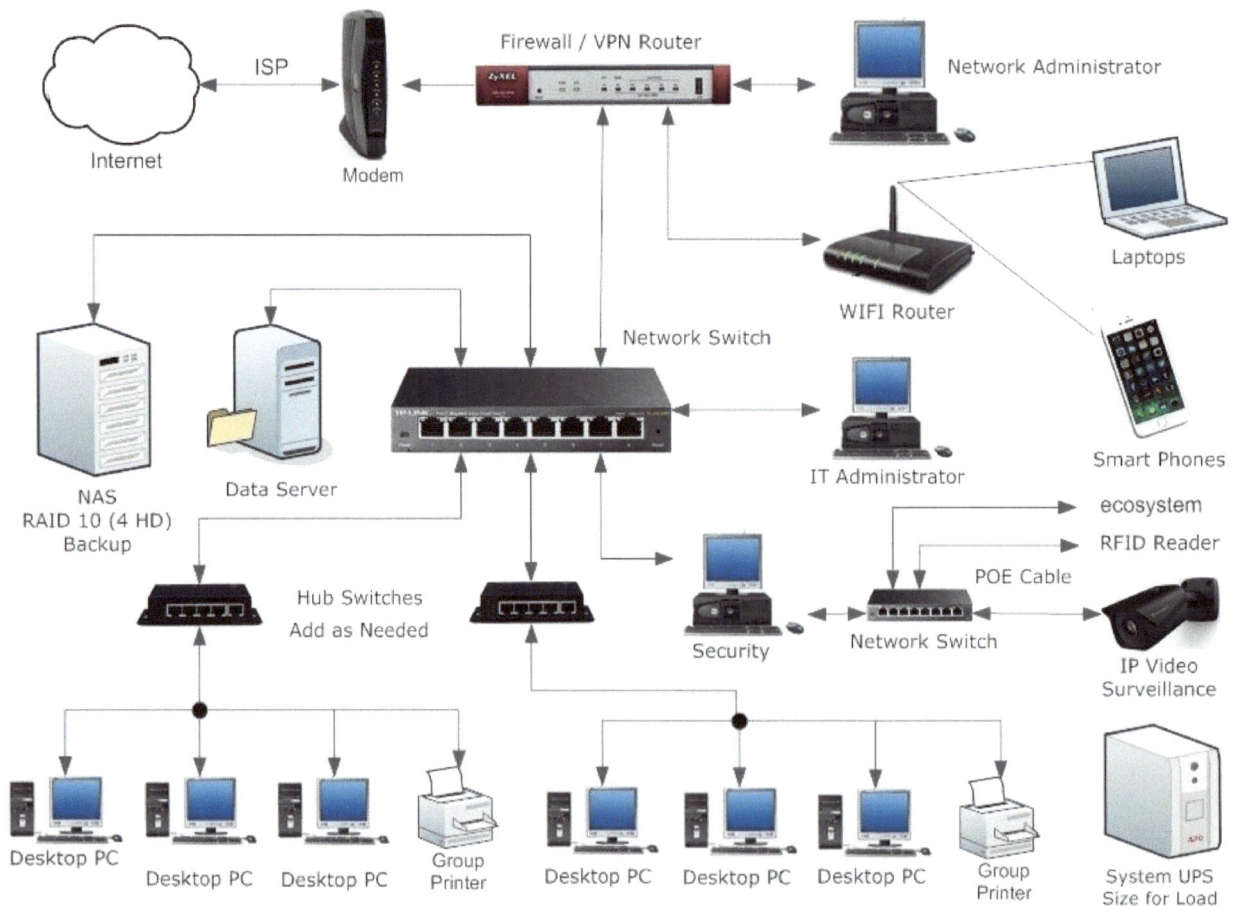

Figure 4.2

Note: Refer to section 12.7.11 titled, "The use of VPN – Virtual Private Networks" Refer to chapter 13 for detailed information on Video/RFID surveillance systems.

Although, the image of the UPS (Uninterruptible Power Supply) in Figure 4.2 is an image of a standalone UPS unit, know that a backup system for an enterprise application is as complex as the Network System Architecture itself and requires careful planning to protect both equipment and data.

4.6   Professional IT Associations

There are scores of Information Technology Associations.   Each has its own niche and many offer certification training. Here's the list of IT Professional Associations & Organizations

ACET (Association of Computer Engineers and Technicians)
AHIMA (American Health Information Management Association
AIIP (Association of Independent Information Professionals)
AITP (Association of Information Technology Professionals)
AMC (Association for Computing Machinery)
ARMA (American Records Management Association)
ASIS International (American Society for Industrial Security)
ASP (Association of Software Professionals)
BICSI (Professional association advancing the information and communications technology)
BIIA (Business Information Industry Association)
CompTIA (Information Technology Industry Association)
HIMSS (Healthcare Information and Management Systems Society)
ICRM (Institute of Certified Records Management)
IHRIM (International Association for Human Resources Information)
IRMS (Information and Records Management)
ISACA (Information Systems Audit and Control Association)
ISSA (Information Systems Security Association)
SAA (Society of American Archivists)
SIM (Society for Information Management)
SIRM (Society for Human Resource Management)

Reference Standards:
ISO 18829:2017
Document management - Assessing ECM/EDRM implementations - Trustworthiness
ISO 22957:2018
Document management - Analysis, selection and implementation of enterprise content management (ECM) systems
ISO 9001:2015 (7.1.6)
Quality management systems - Requirements
ISO 8601-1:2019
Date and time - Representations for information interchange - Part 1: Basic rules
ISO 15489-1:2016
Information and Documentation Records Management - Concepts and Principles
ISO 27001-1:2017
Information technology –Security techniques - Information security management systems - Requirements

SOX - Sarbanes Oxley
FDA - Date Retention (Medical Devices)
PHI - Protected Health Information
PCI DSS - Payment Card Industry Data Security Standards

Chapter 5 – "Property of" Labels

5.0   Overview

When referring to labels for tracking assets a company has two primary options: (1) use of legacy barcode label (with either 1D linear or 2D symbology); or (2), state of the art labels that combine both a barcode with a UHF RFID tag or NFC tag laminated within the label to track assets.

If you go with the 2nd option, you can use a handheld RFID reader, a Sled, or for security RF antennas can be used at all facility entrances and exits to be alerted when a particular asset is taken out of the building. You can then combine that technology with video surveillance.

The latest RFID technology employs triangulation to locate assets in real time, referred to as RTLS (Real Time Location System). People can be tracked within your facility the same way by embedding a UHF RFID tag in their ID badge – used for both visitors and employees. By grouping or classifying assets tracking them by way of an RTLS on each floor or area of your facility can be done right at a computer monitor with RTLS software. By clicking on the marker appearing on the RTLS map details regarding that asset are displayed.

Regardless of the system you employ to track your assets, a "Property of" label is still required to verify the RFID tag applied to the asset and your RFID interrogators are reading the correct tag. The asset label at a minimum should have the number assigned to an asset as well as a corresponding bar code – with either 1D or 2D bar code symbology. The two most popular 1D or linear symbologies are Code 3 of 9 and Code 128 Auto.

5.1   "Property of" Schema

When configuring a schema for an asset label you should think in terms of facilitating the tracking task itself. As we stated in Chapter 2 there are many different types of assets and based on their classification and cost will determine how they will be tracked and either capitalized or expensed, respectfully.

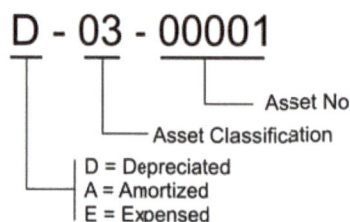

D - 03 - 00001

├──────── Asset No
├──── Asset Classification
├─ D = Depreciated
├─ A = Amortized
└─ E = Expensed

Figure 5.1

The Property Record displayed in Appendix K was programmed to automatically fill the Asset prefixes and record number that appears in the upper right hand corner of that eForm based on the asset's total cost basis and classification. This schema was designed to aid in the task of physically or remotely tracking assets by their respective definition, whether by department, type, or to facilitate cycle audits.

5.2   Printer Types

The most popular bar code printer is a thermal printer which uses roll labels. We used Dymo* and Zebra* thermal printers. Currently paper, polypropylene, and polyester labels are readily available for Dymo*. Those as well as polyimide labels are readily available for Zebra thermal printers.

5.3   Label Materials

There are four types of labels available for thermal printers: (1) paper; (2), polyester; (3), polypropylene; and (4), polyimide.   Polyester also referred to as *Weather Proof* labels are generally accepted for most asset labeling. This label's temperature rating is from -40°C to +150°C.   Refer to 3M* label types 7246 and 7247 and 3M* adhesive type 350.

Polypropylene labels are commonly used for shipping labels as well as for laboratory labels and cryogenic applications that require a temperature range from -196°C to 70°C. Refer to Diversified Biotech labels.

Kapton* DuPont Polyimide labels has the highest temperature rating of -269°C to 400°C and for that reason are commonly used for labeling printed circuit boards and is made to withstand solder reflow processing. Refer to 3M* 7812 thermal transfer labels.

Adhesives: Two types of adhesives are commonly used for asset labels. The most common is an acrylic based adhesive. For more severe environmental conditions a silicone based adhesive is also available. Refer to Adhesion Standard ASTM D 3330.

Compliance Standards: There are two Mil standards when referring to asset labels and marking – MIL STD129 and MIL STD 130 as well as MIL STD 883.

Note: All labels have at least two characteristics that determine their application rating – the plastic substrate and the adhesive. Therefore they must be de-rated accordingly based on the supplier's specifications for practical use.

5.4   Barcode Symbologies

There are many different types of 1D linear bar code symbologies, each developed and compliant for its use and particular industry. Code 128 and Code 3 of 9 are the most commonly used in manufacturing. As you can see Code 128 Auto is able to contain the same data in a smaller space or width and for that reason is favored in the electronics manufacturing industry, especially for PCB labels.

Figure 5.2

The 2D QR Code barcode, as it appears, contains the same asset number as the two 1D barcode examples, but is capable of containing multiple lines of data. However, it requires a 2D reader. 2D readers are capable of reading 1D or linear barcodes as well. Barcode scanners are also universal in their ability to read a number of specified barcode symbologies. The manufacturer of the scanner normally provides a list of symbologies each device is capable of reading. Scanners are also either corded or uncorded or both. Refer to section 12.7.8 regarding security concerns related to *Bluetooth* devices and Dongles.

By incorporating the text identifier directly under the barcode when performing an audit the person charged with that task can quickly see if the asset matches the list given without the need to use a barcode scanner.

5.5   RFID Tags & Readers (Interrogators)

There are different types of RFID tags, each with their own characteristics. In this section we'll cover various types since they can be commonly embedded in a *Property of* label. There are other types of RTLS tracking devices such as UWB (Ultrawide Band) and BLE (Bluetooth Low Energy) beacons; however, they are normally separate from a *Property of* label and will covered instead in Chapter 6 titled, "Tracking Methods".

5.5.1   Type by Frequency & Range

When categorizing RFID tags by signal frequency they break down into three basic types, and as listed are capable of being detected by a corresponding reader or interrogator at a greater distance:

LF – 125 kHz

This is similar to a NFC (Near Field Communication) tag, meaning the tag needs to be very close to a reader like those devices used in a *Point of Sale* application – normally only a cm away. Also called bump tags.

HF - 13.56 MHz (FCC assigned Industrial/Scientific Bandwidth)

This tag has a limited range and is normally used in an application where the subject asset or person must walk through or by a narrow gate or exit in order for the reader to detect the signal or via a hand held reader. Near Field Communication (NFC) tags can also operate at this frequency – normally a few feet away. NFC tags are capable of being encoded (write) and decoded (read) by the same device – like a cell phone or tablet with the proper App. Some handheld Tablets have NFC transreceiver or can read NFC data via internal Bluetooth or with a dongle.

NFC 13.56 MHz
Read Distance Approx. 5cm
Figure 5.3

UHF – Although the frequency range for UHF is generally defined as from 300 MHz and 3 GHz, UHF RFID tags are more commonly available in the frequency range of 860-960MHZ. This type of tag is the most common for RTLS, capable of being detected 20 meters away or longer, depending the strength of the RF antenna and/or reader. These tags are relatively inexpensive and can be supplied with adhesive backing on rolls for about $0.50 each. The characteristics to look for are: die size, reading distance, and write data storage time in years. Distance is usually dependent on the RF antenna or reader, but the tag distance is also a factor. Based on the current state-of-the-art, if you expect to have a UHF tag be read 30-50 feet away the size of that tag is at least 2.75" in length and 0.75" wide - the smaller the tag, the shorter the range. Range has to do with many environmental conditions, but distance has more to do with the gain of the UHF readers.

UHF RFID 840-960 MHz
Read Distance Approx. 30 ft.
Figure 5.4.

UWB – Defined as Ultra-Wide-Bandwidth RFID tags operate in the GHz range – up to about 10.6GHz. Generally they have a far greater range than UHF RFID tags. More expensive Active or battery powered UWB tags may use UWB/BLE Radio for Precise Indoor Positioning sensor technology and are even programmable. For that reason UWB are gaining popularity for RTLS applications in large warehouses.

Note: If you're developing or re-designing a tagging system and in addition to a barcode you are considering a label with an embedded HF NFC or UHF RFID tag you need to project your needs into the future. For example, long range Passive UHF RFID tags may work with a RTLS under ideal conditions and with the right readers or antennas, but Passive UWB may work better. This is due to plant layout (obstructions) or the type of business you operate. A Near Field Communication tag works with a handheld reader only.

Combination Barcode RFID Tag
Figure 5.5

5.5.2   Active vs Passive Tags
There are actually three main types: (1), Active; (2), Passive; and (3), Semi-Passive.

Active This tag is referred to as "Active" due to the fact it includes a battery. These typically have a longer range, but battery life is an issue.

Passive This tag is referred to as Passive and has no battery. It relies on the signal from the reader to supply whatever current is necessary by creating a magnetic field to relay a signal back to the reader.

BAP   This tag is defined as a *Battery Assisted Passive* tag, also referred to as a *Semi-Passive* tag. Like an *Active* tag, it has a longer range than a *Passive* tag, but again there is the issue of battery life. A BAP tag can also be supplied with integrated sensors to report temperature and other conditions important, for example, in the food industry.

Class: *Class 0* is a UHF read only passive tag. *Class 1* is passive read & write or *WORM* (*Write Once Read Many*) tag. *Class 2* is a passive tag that can be written to at any point in the supply chain. *Class 3* is either an Active or Semi-Passive read write tag with sensors capable of recording environmental conditions. *Class* 4 is a read-write tag with a transmitter that can communicate with other tags and readers. *Class 5* is similar to a Class 4 tag, but can provide power to other tags and can communicate with devices other than readers.

5.5.3   Type by Compliance Standard – Gen 1 vs Gen 2 Tags
Gen 1 is an old protocol no longer used. Gen 2 is an *Air Interface Protocol* published by EPC in 2004. EPC (Electronic Product Code) is the trade name associated with the ISO/IEC 18000-6C RFID standards. In 2008 the Gen 2 version 1.2.1 protocol was published and is still widely used in most systems.

5.5.4   Features in upcoming EPC Class Gen 2 Version 2 Tags
Currently Gen 2 Version 2 is pending final publication. This new version is expected to have superior security features and ad ed flexibility over its Gen 2 Version 1.2.1 predecessor. Here's an advance release of those new features:

Anti-counterfeiting Measures:
Authenticate a tag as genuine. This feature will ensure that no tags can be faked as each tag will have the ability to respond by using a stored secret key.

Security:
This feature will allow you to modify tag informa tion securely. User memory banks can only be accesses based on privilege. That privilege includes reading, writing, and locking.

File Management:
Currently with Gen 2 Version 1.2.1 tags all memory is in one file. The new version 2.0 allows the user to create multiple files separate from each other in the same memory bank and assign access privilege to each while hiding other files as an item moves through the supply chain or is processed.

Untraceability:
The new version tag can hide tag data to protect privacy. Concern parts of the memory bank can be hidden which has great promise in retail, ID cards, and for healthcare.

Loss Prevention:
This feature can be used in EAS (Electronic Article Surveillance) by including a store and sold code on each RFID tag so the business will know if the item left sold or stolen when the tag is read.

Note: Obviously, some of these features have benefits for Asset Management and some not so much. However, these new features leave room for processing creativity. Its primary application is with *Class 2* tags as assets move through the supply chain and processed at the receiving dock – prior to inspection and placing it into service.

5.6   Writing to RFID Tag

Typically, an organization when using RFID tags will use only one type of tag, whether that is NFC/HF, UHF, or UWB. As mentioned earlier HFC/HF tags with their short reading distances lend themselves to Point of Sa es applications, where UHF and UWB tags lend themselves to longer range applications. UWB tags lend themselves to very long distances, but readability in all cases depends on the reader and its gain measure in dbiC. The "C" stands for Circular polarized isotropic radiator. Each requires its own compatible writing device. Here's an example of a UHF Reader/Writer that includes software and an SDK (Software Development Kit) for unique EPC identification schemas:

Figure 5.6 (Courtesy of Fongwah)

Note: This particular model UHF RFID Tag reader/writer is also referred to as a Desktop reader/writer. It can be placed on a workstation desk, using a desktop computer and with compatible application software can be used to write unique EPC IDs to each tag before the Asset is placed into service in a designated location within your facility. Refer to the sample Property Record displayed in Appendix K where that EPC code is recorded. Again, where UWB tags are popular for RTLS that may require very long transmission distances to a reader, such as in a large warehouse, where UHF tags can be used for RTLS applications in smaller spaces they are commonly used in facility portals or exits and/or with handheld readers for asset management audits or inventory control. UHF tags are available with WORM (Write Once Read Many) features or those that can be protect from unauthorized change via passwords.

Chapter 6 – Tracking Methods

6.0   Overview – Legacy Barcode, RFID, UWB, BLE, & GPS

The Property Record, like the one displayed in Appendix K is key to determining how each asset is classified and categorized for tracking. A plan for tracking or performing an audit cannot be efficiently done without this completed recordset. From this recordset a spreadsheet listing of specific assets can be generated to be included in each cycle audit or inventory of assets. This is the case regardless whether you are using a legacy method of tracking assets with only barcode labels or using a state of the art RFID RTLS (Real Time Location System). As you can see from the Figure 6.1 in section 6.1.2 without first categorizing all assets an RTLS map could get too crowded with tag markers to locate any specific asset.

RFID is actually a technology that is now decades old. However, even though there are other asset locating devices and technology introduced more recently, RFID still remains the most popular technology mainly due to the cost of the UHF RIFID tags and RTLS. When the industry makes available Gen 2 Version 2 tags and support software with its additional security and flexibility, RFID should be here to stay for a long while. To stay current with advancements in RFID technology refer to https://www.rfidjournal.com/

Other technologies introduced more recently include UWB (Ultrawide Band) and BLE (Bluetooth Low Energy) devices and apps. UWB can operate from 3.1 GHz to 10.6 GHz. It is FCC Part 15.250 and ETSI EN 302 500-1 compliant. The international standards for UWB are IEEE 802.15.4.f and ISO-24730-61 (currently in draft form). BLE, formerly called Bluetooth Smart operates at 2.4 GHz. Bluetooth SIG (Special Interest Group) is the standards organization. Although, UWB and BLE asset locating devices and supporting technology have advantages, like longer range detection, similar to Active RFID tags, their uses are limited. However, major players in the industry like Zebra and others have moved into these new markets.

Both UWB and BLE devices are battery powered, are larger in size, and more expensive than UHF RFID tags. UWB is known to be more accurate with respect to pinpointing location. Prices currently run between $15 to $25 and more, where UHF (Long Range) RFID tags are readily available for $0.50 or less.

Finally, the last type of tracking method is via GPS. GPS devices are usually installed in vehicles and heavy equipment brought to job sites. The technology commonly employed to track such assets; although, still considered *Asset Management*, it's also called *Fleet Management* and the tracking technology in this sector is referred to as *Telematics*. It can employ RFID and GPS. *Telematics* covers not only asset location but also logistics. This tracking technology is covered in more detail in sections 6.5 and 10.2.7.

6.1   Location Methods

The task of actually locating assets within a facility or a number of facilities can be done primarily using two methods: (1) grid maps; and (2) using a RTLS (Real Time Location System) by labeling assets with UHF RFID tags and then categorizing them so you can see them clearly on a computer monitor from a remote location.

6.1.1   Grid Maps

If you're using a legacy tracking method (without RTLS) then you will need to prepare a 2D illustration of each floor or department within your facility and divide those layout drawings with coded grid zones. If your business has more than one site of operation then a designator for each site location should be included in your coding schema. As you can see from the Grid Map Schema in Figure 6.1 we use the same factory site identifier as used in our LTC (Lot Trace Code).

If you are a growing company, in addition to a factory site location you may want to include designators for building number, floor or department, and the grid location where that asset is in place. So a schema for GLC (*Grid Location Code*) may look something like this:

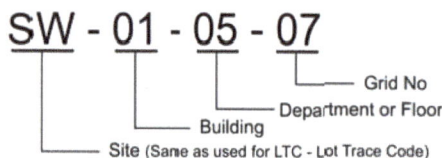

Figure 6.1

In addition to a GLC, to facilitate the task of taking an inventory of existing assets you will need a floor plan layout of the subject area with an overlay displaying divisions and grid designations. As you can see the floor plan is grayed so the grid can be more easily seen. Careful thought should be put into grid division. Depending on the size of your operations, facility, the floor layout drawings, and grid divisions, it may be more complex. Obviously, the GLC will only work for assets that are categorized as Stationary. Mobile assets will need alternative means of tracking based on their category and how they are used. Normally the employee tasked with the audit will load what they need onto an electronic tablet, along with a barcode scanner or perhaps a RF D sled with smart phone or handheld RFID reader. RFID handheld readers have the advantage of finding assets within several meters regardless where their *Property-of* labels are affixed. Normally, an Excel spreadsheet will be prepared in advance as well with the subject assets sorted by GLC, making the task easier. This data can be exported from the Property Recordset into a spreadsheet or database and then to a Asset Tracker like the one displayed in Appendix P.

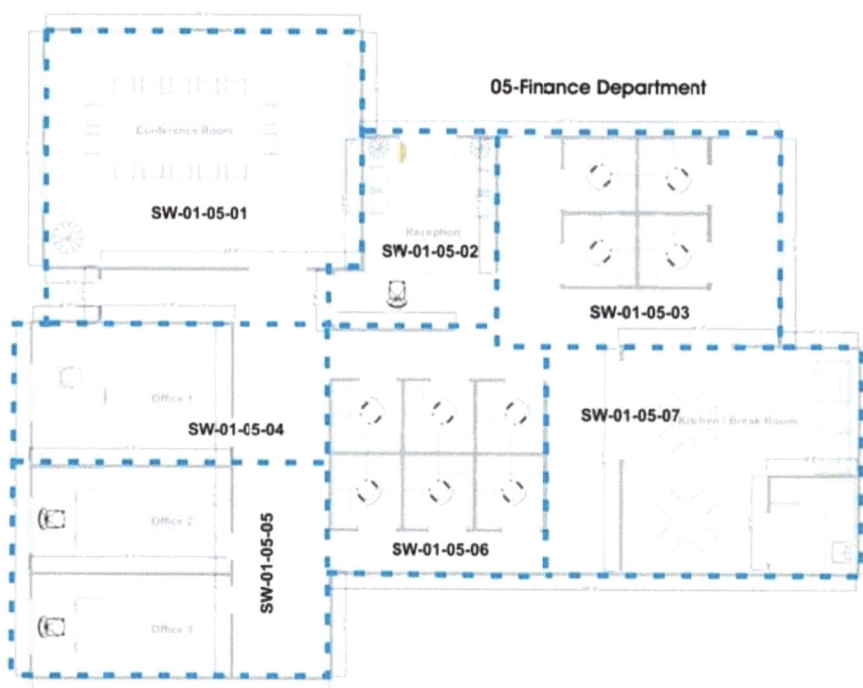

Figure 6.2

At the very least you will still need a floor plan layout for a RTLS program. RTLS software will normally have some means to bring a floor plan into view so assets can be located and identified with map markers superimposed on a floor plan layout drawing.

6.1.2 RFID Signal Triangulation and RTLS

To protect and track assets you can use RFID tags and readers to alert you when assets are carried out of your facilities pass an exit, like the *Nox* System that combines video and RFID surveillance, originally developed for the FBI and now commercially available by SimplyRFID, and/or track assets in real time as a means to take an inventory or even check on the status of an asset with respect to *Preventative Maintenance* events or other real time data. The ladder is referred to as a RTLS (Real Time Location System). This can be especially useful with equipment that rolls around on the floor, making it perfect for medical facilities.

By categorizing assets you can employ RTLS software to take inventory and the markers on the map below can be tagged to pull up property numbers and other data specific to the asset:

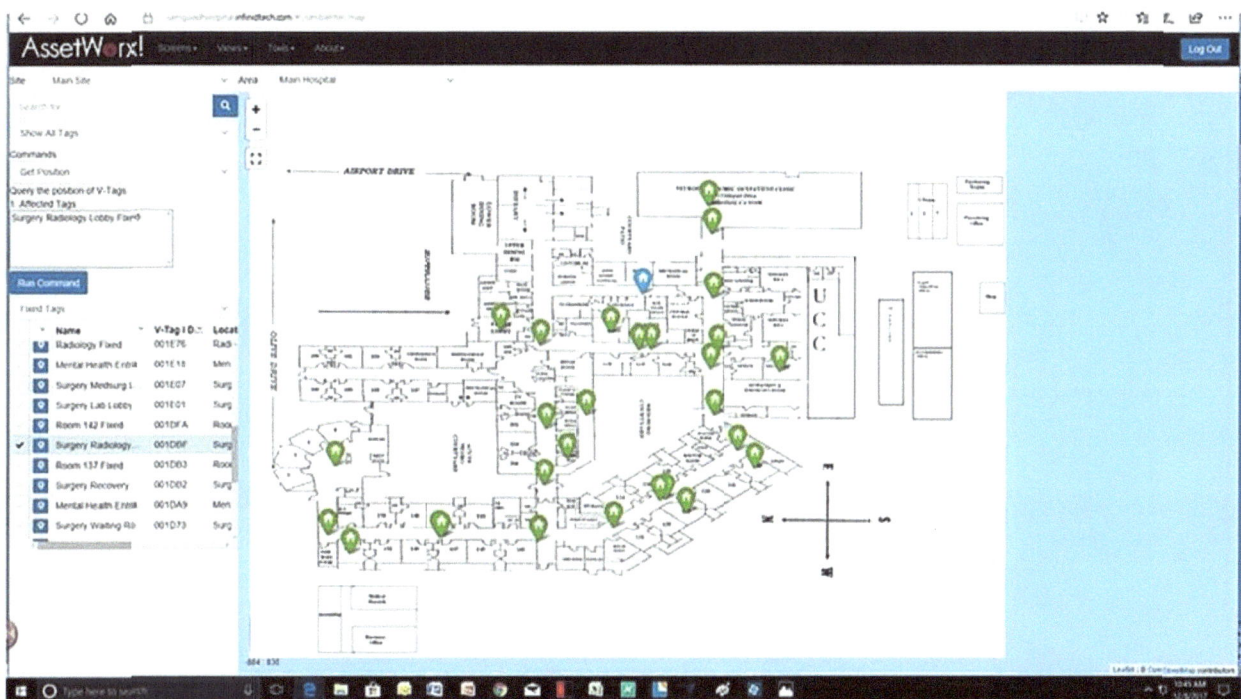

Courtesy of InfinID Technologies Inc.

Figure 6.3

6.2 Tracking Devices

The first order of business when adopting a system for tracking assets is to decide whether to opt for barcode or RFID or a combination of both. The next order of business is to decide whether to use a single line of data to capture only the Property No. or multiple lines of data using a 2D barcode or RFID, also capable of storing multiple lines of data. Then, if you go with multiple lines of data, you need to decide what data to store. You can always set your device to capture only the key line or Property No. and only use the additional lines of data on your reader to confirm or double-check against what's stored on your master database or spreadsheet.

The Excel template displayed in Appendix N only requires the key in order to Autofill all other data on the Asset Tracker eform corresponding to the key. It uses an updated master ODBC compliant database or spreadsheet to retrieve that data. Once of key is scanned or read the other data Autofills down to the word CONDITION. All data below that point is recorded as the audit is conducted. The filename for data transfer employed is the DCR assigned Form No. The FAB code sends the data to a specified folder as well.

Again, the advantage of RFID is that it is not necessary to have enough space for a line of sight reading of a barcode label, you only need to point to capture key data – Property No. Further, most RFID handheld readers are set to a limited range in order to ensure you receive only the signal data from the asset item you are pointing the device at.

Also, regardless what method or device you employ, that data will have to be stored on either a cell phone with an App or a tablet. Tablets are readily available with an Android OS, but if you're using Formdocs* or a PC workstation with a Windows OS then its best you also use a Tablet running on a Windows7, 8, or 10 so you can transfer that Tablet stored data after an audit to your workstation PC in order to produce reports from the collection of Asset Tracker records displayed in Appendix P. Appendix Q displays the FAB script programmed into our Asset Tracker eform in order to generate a report in Excel in specified data columns. See the report in Appendix N. You can use filters in Excel or your database to pull out separate reports for assets that have gone missing or reached their end of life, to prepare for write-downs, disposal, or sale.

When searching for a reliable Windows Tablet, we prefer nothing any larger than an 8 inch model. They range in price from $75 to $600 and more. One designed for enterprise use, and capable of daily abuse may be your best choice. You'll need a pouch with a belt clip and you may want to consider a wall mounted biometric lockbox otherwise scanners, RFID readers, and writers may go missing when not in use.

6.2.1   Barcode Scanners

Most people in business know what a barcode scanner looks like. Today they come in all shapes and sizes, but we advise to purchase one capable of reading 1D and 2D symbologies. Most 2D scanners are also capable of reading 1D-symbologies as well. Here's example of a 1D/2D scanner:

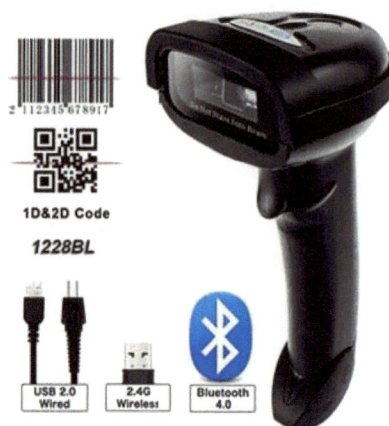

Figure 6.4 *(Courtesy of Netum)*

Note: This model is capable of scanning with Wireless employing Bluetooth or with a USB cable. Some companies prohibit the use of Bluetooth for security reasons. The goes for RFID readers as well. You'll need to attach the Dongle to your Tablet and/or your PC when employing Bluetooth. At the very least make sure you remove the USB Dongle from your Tablet or PC workstation when you're done using it. Refer to Section 12 for more information regarding security practices.

6.2.2   Handheld RFID readers

Of course, there are wall mount RFID antennas and readers for recording time stamps as asset items come and go through portals or exits in your facility, preferably combined with video surveillance at those exits, but for taking inventory or performing a periodic audit of assets a handheld device is the most practical approach for many companies or organizations.

6.2.3   Handheld RFID "Sled"

There is an UHF RFID reader commonly referred to as a "Sled", meaning it's designed so you can slide a smart phone or dedicated tablet with an App that communicates with the reader below via Bluetooth. Some companies prefer not to use employee's cell phones for such purpose or store data on an employee's cell phone, so in such case a dedicated tablet may be preferable. There are tablets for "Sled" readers that include barcode scanning capabilities as well. Here's an example of a popular "Sled" RFID reader.

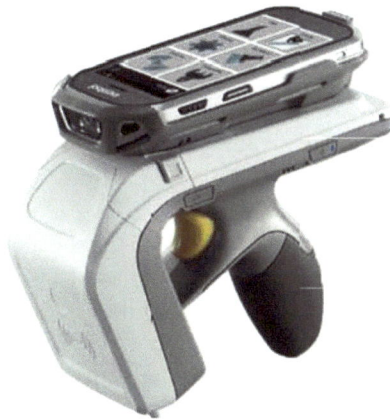

Figure 6.5 *(Courtesy of Zebra)*

6.2.4   Handheld Combination RFID Reader/Barcode Scanner

This one displayed here is a miniature multiple use device capable of both reading UHF RFID tags and scanning 1D and 2D barcodes. It also has a convenient strap which allows the user to pick up asset or inventory or close your hand to press the button to activate the RFID reader or scanner.

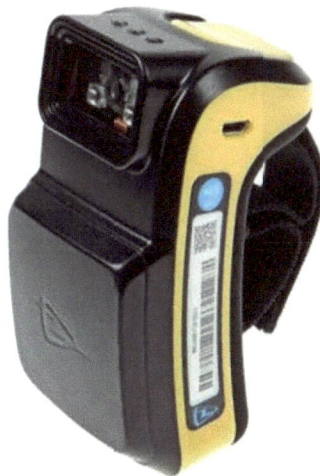

Figure 6.6 *(Courtesy of TLS* Technology Solutions UK)*

6.3   Categorizing Assets

To ease the task of taking an inventory of assets it will be necessary to categorize them. Viewing the screen captured image above in Figure 6.3 of this RTLS program, you can see how difficult it would be to find assets on this superimposed floor layout without sorting and then selecting the categories in the column to the left, one category at a time. It would be even more difficult with a legacy barcode system, relying on map grids.

The *Property Record* is the one place to record the proper category for each asset based on the *Directives* provided for that task. Further, so far we have used the terms type, asset class, category, and group. Let's define each term to promote a clearer understanding:

> **Type**: This term refers to the cost recovery method: Depreciation, Amortization, or Expensed. Tangible asset items, if capitalized are depreciated and intangible items are amortized, like software and/or rights provided by written agreements.

> **Class**: This term can mean a lot of things, but for our purposes here the term means the classes detailed in the appendices of IRS Publication 946 in the MACRS tables and as listed in Chapter 2, section 2.4 for computers, office furniture, plant machinery, or tooling.

> **Category**: With this term we will refer to whether once placed in service it is stationary or mobile.

> **Group**: This term will be used to define how mobile assets are managed and tracked by group.

6.3.1   Capitalized vs Expensed

We have already explained in Chapter 2, section 2.2 how to determine whether an asset is either capitalized or expensed and how to set the limit with respect to cost basis to make such determination. This has more to do with accounting and how to depreciate, amortize, or expense an asset than it does with tracking those assets. When tracking capitalized assets you are auditing to determine if your balance sheet is an accurate representation of cost and the prevailing book value. When recording an expense or even a period deduction after depreciation or amortization, it is important to know in what account to record that expense; for example, whether to charge manufacturing, administration, marketing, or product development.

This is usually reflected in the *Depreciation & Amortization Detail Sheet* where the cost of assets, period deductions, and book value are sub-totaled to correspond to the organization's Profit & Loss Statement as well as its Balance Sheet. This is why when an asset is transferred from one department to another that transfer should be recorded on an Asset Disposition Report and provided to accounting.

How well you detail your GL (General Ledger) and Chart of Accounts will determine to a great extent the level of control you're able to maintain over your operations, or the quality of your BI (Business Intelligence). In other words, before you can generate *Dashboards* that can help management make decisions, the source of data must be specific. On the other hand, more account detail than you need given your business model and its size can be a unnecessary burden. This is why when designing a *Chart of Accounts*, consecutive account numbers are skipped so they can be added when growth warrants more detail.

6.3.2   Stationary vs Mobile Assets

The other provision on the Property Record is to record whether an asset is either *Stationary* or *Mobile*. If the asset is *Stationary* in most cases it does not move after it is placed in service. However, if an asset is *Mobile* both managing and tracking that asset becomes more difficult.

6.4   Tracking Mobile Assets by Group

In addition to provisions on the Property Record to record *Type*, *Class*, and *Category* we then have to *Group* each *Mobile* asset so it can be managed and tracked. We covered this to some degree in Chapter 3 in section 3.14, 3.16, 3.17, and 3.18. Based on how these assets are used and by who will normally determine into which group they will fall:

Tool Crib: In section 3.16 we covered the use of a *Tool Crib Receipt* to track consignment and return of mobile assets. This is actually the primary point from which all mobile assets are first received and assigned. Some assets are consigned to employees and returned daily or when the job is done and others are assigned to department heads where once consigned they are kept in locked cabinets within those departments (i.e. HR or Production). Where it is not practical to have employees line up and wait every morning in front of the *Tool Crib,* those mobile assets are normally stored in locked work station drawers or in locked vehicles (i.e. in case of field service vehicles).

The vehicles themselves are typically managed and tracked by **Fleet Managers** as are the assets inside. Before field vehicles are reassigned an inventory of assets within should be taken by Fleet Management.

The **Tool Crib Manager** may be assigned the duty of applying barcoded *Property-of* labels to mobile assets or even be tasked with writing identifying asset data to a UHF RFID tag affixed under the barcode label. This will require a small desktop RFID reader/writer device and a desktop computer. A **Property Manager** or **Facilities Manager** may be assigned to affix *Property-of* labels and RFID tags to all stationary assets. **Fleet Managers** are typically tasked with affixing labels and installing GPS devices for tracking purposes prior to vehicles being placed in service or assigned. Whoever applies the asset labels should also complete at least key parts of the Property Record.

The **Tool Crib** is also an ideal place to store combination accessories or repeat/disposable items for various assets (i.e. toner cartridges, paper, etc.). By keeping supplies in one location the Tool Crib manager can track use and flag purchasing when the last or last few supply items are left in stock. Minimum inventory of supplies can be established by rate of use. All supply items for assets should be identified by make and model number on the asset's Property Record. See Appendix K.

If any production department's locked cabinets are used to store hard tooling a record of units of production should be maintained on a log to flag management when tool repair or new tooling is required. See class 34.01 assets under the IRS MACRS depreciation tables.

Normal practice is to call back all workstation kits for inspection when the employee leaves the company or organization – for office and production. When new department heads start work an inventory of their locked departmental cabinets is taken, the log checked, and new lock codes are issued. Logs should also be kept for all departmental cabinets date and time stamped as assets are removed for use and returned.

Assets stored in the locked HR department are typically assigned to new employees or those promoted into new positions and employees acknowledge receipt by their signature. See section 3.17 and Appendix S, Part 1. When an employee leaves employment, during the Exit Interview return of assets listed on HR- Consigned Asset Record must be returned before any remaining wages or severance pay are paid out. Those returns are confirmed when HR signs off on the form in Appendix S, Part 2 mentioned in section 3.18. This becomes the employee's proof of return. Copies of both forms should be kept in the Employee's HR jacket, along with all other employment records for that employee. Preparation of those assets may include writing identifying data to an RFID card affixed to the employee's badge.

So to recap, all mobile assets are originally distributed from the ***Tool Crib.*** Others are kept in locked ***workstation drawers***, ***departmental cabinets***, or if ***field service vehicles*** are used, in those vehicles under lock and key. Small companies may combine ***Inventory Stores*** and ***Tool Crib*** operations; although, we recommend separating the two as soon as it is practical. For example, in electronic manufacturing receiving and kitting from stores is normally a full time job.

6.5   Use of Cycle Methods
The 80/20 rule is typically employed to define Class A, B, and C inventory when referring to raw materials and components for production. Cycle audits or tracking asset inventory may employ first categorizing and/or grouping assets before preparing a plan for audits via cycling methods. How you approach managing audits of assets may be based on the size or nature of your business. Any audit practices related to financial reporting should be established with written policies and remain constant until that policy is changed.

6.6   GIS Infrastructure Mapping & Tracking
GIS stands for Geographic Information System. Typically, it works as follows: when infrastructure assets are buried or fixed in place such as cable, pipes, and/or traffic signals the GPS location is recorded. This information is entered into GIS software and those marked locations appear over a geographical map. Each marker includes make, model, and serial number as well as the date it was installed, along with other information. Based on each asset's expected useful life the software provides reports of dates for repair or replacement along with either maintenance or replacement cost for budgetary purposes. This software is commonly used by public works departments within municipalities and other government entities, port authorities, or any entity with such assets.

If the items are buried, when work crews go out to maintain or replace those assets, RFID tags buried over those assets help those crews know where to dig. The depth of those RFID tags may depend on the soil conditions. In addition to the RFID tags EMS tape is often employed to locate the path of the cable or pipe. The GIS re ders resemble a handheld metal detector with a data acquisition screen on top as follows:

Figure 6.7 *(Locating & Marking System Courtesy of 3M)*

6.7   Asset Disposition

Now that we've covered the various methods of tracking assets based on category, what happens if you discover an asset item falls into one of these disposition codes?

A) Asset Transferred – to another department or grid zone location
B) Gone Missing – either stole or lost
C) Reached its end of useful life – then either processed for sale or donation
D) Not Working – needs repair -including PM service
E) Impairment – meaning, damaged in fire or due to some other event

These disposition codes can be entered on the *Asset Tracker* eForm while taking inventory via an electronic tablet or laptop. See Appendix P. These are all events in which an *Asset Disposition Report* is required. When using relational database recordsets all data from *Property Records* should be exported to an Excel spreadsheet or ODBC compliant database, listing assets to be audited sorted by grid map locations. Using *Autofill*, as you enter the assigned *Property Numbers* using the barcode, the description, make, model, and serial number of that asset should appear automatically on that *Asset Disposition Report* record. The *Asset Tracker* can also be autofilled using ODBC compliant databases. From there, you can follow whatever *Directives* are in place to communicate your findings so appropriate follow-up action can be taken.

Typically, stationary assets should not be moved or transferred to another department or location without first notifying management, accounting, a Property Manager, or a Facility Manager.   Most companies or organizations have a policy in place that requires employees and department heads to notify management as soon as asset go missing – at least on the day it is discovered missing.

Also, the employee tasked with taking inventory should be instructed to ask those working within each designated grid zone being audited if they know of any equipment within their area has gone missing or needs service. If anyone should know, it would be those who have to use the zone assets on a regular basis. It should be made clear that all employees are expected to cooperate during such audits.

The best place to communicate policies like this is to include it in the *Employee Handbook.* It should also be made clear in their handbook or *Employment Agreement*, if they don't follow the policies set forth, it will affect their performance review.

Note: When assets fall under disposition codes C, D, & E they are typically moved to a quarantined area where follow-up action can be taken, with their Asset Disposition form attached. As a matter of practice various employees tasked with specific follow-up actions are notified with a copy of the Asset Disposition eForm. IT should prepare email folders to store **Routed** communications and Directives should be drafted to instruct process participants as to their use. If PM service is required on stationary assets then service can be done in place when practical.

6.8   Tracking Exclusion List Based on Risk Assessment

First, regardless whether an asset is capitalized, expensed, or placed on a risk assessment exclusion list, it should always be labeled with a Property-of label and/or RFID tag. If you're a private enterprise and you decide to expense everything with a cost basis less than $2,500 you may wish to list assets, for example, that have a cost basis less than $200.00 not to be tracked due to a low risk of loss.

In such cases the man hour cost of tracking or taking inventory of such assets may cost more than what a company experiences in yearly loss of such assets. However, it would be far better to prepare such a list by type and risk of loss. Some assets are typically used daily and therefore monitored every day by employees.

For example, if an employee comes in on Monday morning and finds his or her desktop PC, keyword, monitor, and/or mouse missing from their workstation, you know it will be reported immediately. Of course, the only way you're going to track and trend such loses is to generate a Deposition Report when such items go missing or reach their end-of-life, along with any other assets of higher value.

However, other small assets like handheld instruments, only used occasionally are more at risk of loss so they need to be tracked or audited on a periodic basis.

In Washington the State Auditor refers to assets under $5,000 which are required by law to be expensed, as "Small and Attractive Assets". The State also publishes a manual referred to as the State Administrative and Accounting Manual (SAAM). As stated in section 30.40.20 a city may adopt a policy if in writing that excuses it from tracking specific types of assets that, for example cost less than $300 or $1,000 when falling into two categories by type per section 30.40.20 and the charts that appear in that section of the manual.

In other words, based on documented experience if a state or local government entity can demonstrate the cost in man hours to take inventory of such assets cost more than the risk of loss of those asset types, tracking can be excluded from periodic internal audits, especially when in effect employees audit assets they use every day. However, the state sets two thresholds for various types of small assets in its SAAM. So, thresholds limits are set by the state and discretion is left to the state auditors when it feels the list of excluded assets is overdone.

Say you have $100,000 worth of very small assets that cost less than $300 each of a particular type that would cost $3,000 in man hours to track, but reports can demonstrate loss of those items is less than $500 annually and loss would be discovered immediately during the normal course of operations. Therefore, it would make little sense to track them. If you did, you'd lose money with each audit.

HOWEVER, each department head should be required to fill out a Disposition Report otherwise operational records will soon not match accounting records, especially for those expensed assets. The Disposition Reports help quantify lost assets, end-of-life, flag need for maintenance, to determine loss, and establish departmental budgets for replacement.

Government entities in Washington State must also follow the *Budgeting, Accounting, and Reporting System* (BARS) manual as well as GASB. Other states may have guidance manuals with different titles. Check with your state regulatory agencies for similar guidance.

Chapter 7 – Cost Basis

7.0 Overview

A lot of business owners think that *Net Cost* of an asset appearing on an Invoice is the *Cost Basis*. Fact is, cost includes net amount, freight, sales tax, and even any installation cost. So, for example, if you purchase an asset and its *Net Cost* is just under the *IRS Safe Harbor* limit of $2,500, but freight, sales tax, and/or the cost of installation cause the total amount or *Cost Basis* to go over that limit, you'll be required to depreciate the total amount. Again, without *Applicable* (audited) financial statements $2,500 or less is optional for a private company as long as the limit is set by policy and consistent; on the other hand, municipalities or other government entities are required to use the full current $5,000 limit according to GASB. For further information refer to IRS publication 551 titled, "Basis of Assets". Refer to Appendix J.

7.1 Components of Cost Basis

Here's a typical calculation of total Cost Basis related to a purchase of plant equipment:

Net Invoice Amount	$ 2,495.00
Freight	120.00
Sales Tax	274.58
Sub Total	$ 2,889.58
Bringing electrical service to machine	800.00
Installation	250.00
Local Inspection Sticker	125.00
Total Cost Basis	$ 4,064.58

7.2 Increase in Basis

Costs to simply repair or maintain an equipment item or asset to its normal state of functionality is treated as an operating expense. However, repairs and replacements that cost over the amount you have set or required to capitalize can be capitalized if it increases the usefulness and/or efficiency of the asset.

An example, with respect to an amortized intangible asset like a patent, would be if you had to spend money to defend that patent or claims within it; for example, during an interference action. Depending on the final outcome you could either increase the cost basis or decrease it. To determine exactly how much you add or subtract from the asset value we recommend you consult with your CPA.

7.3 Decrease in Basis - Impairment

A common impairment would be in case of fire, theft, vandalism, or damage due to some other unforeseen event. However, impairment occurs only when the decrease in value is not recoverable.

A less common example of impairment would be damage due to a "hard tool die" due to misuse which had a projected useful life just before the incident where that asset was good for another 7,500 production parts. However, after die repair was now only good for a projected 1,500 production parts. Based on GAAP the impairment is calculated based on it reduction in useful life. The value is decreased by 6,000 production parts or more if the tool reaches its end of life sooner.

Under the IRS MACRS tables if the cost of production tooling under class 34.01 is recovered in three years, then the impairment must be reflected on the books based on the prevailing IRS rules regarding such impairment. Again, we advise you consult with your CPA.

Chapter 8 – Methods of Depreciation & Amortization

8.0   Overview

As mentioned in the preface there are two types of depreciation and amortization: (1), is required by the IRS referred to as MACRS (Modified Accelerated Cost Recovery System) detailed in IRS Publication 946; and (2), the GAAP (Generally Accepted Accounting Practices) required by FASB, sometimes referred to as the "Book Method". AND yes, this does require you keep two sets Depreciation & Amortization Schedules – one for IRS returns based on MACRS tables and one based on FASB.

8.1   GAAP (Book Method)

Unlike the MACRS method which uses the chart in IRS Publication 946, Appendix A & B, the GAAP or Book Method depreciates the asset over the years it is expected to be in use and includes a residual or "Salvation" value at the end of that useful life, typically 10 - 30% at which time the company is required to report a loss or gain based on that residual amount plus any remaining Net of Amortization amount on the books at the time.   There are basically four different methods of depreciation permitted under GAAP:

8.1.1   Straight Line

With the "Straight Line" method the Cost Basis amount is divided by the number of years the asset is expected to be in use, plus a residual amount for Salvation Value. When amortizing Intangible Assets, GAAP requires you employ the Straight Line method. Assets like patents, or product trademarks, you simply divide by either its useful or lawful life. Useful life, if you can demonstrate the respective product has a shorter life than the protection in years granted by the patent or trademark. When accounting for cost recovery of licensing agreements, and/or contracts that schedule is determined based on the term of such agreements. Also, when Intangible Assets reach their end of life typically there is no salvage value, unless the contract includes a clause to renew for some extended period of time.

8.1.2   DDB – Double Declining Balance

GAAP permits an accelerated method of cost recovery and the DDB method is one of the most popular. This method is computed by dividing "100%" of the Cost Basis by the number of years in the asset's useful life, this is your straight-line depreciation rate. Then, multiply that number by 2 and that is your Double-Declining Depreciation Rate. In this method, depreciation continues until the asset value declines to its salvage value. The formula is: =DDB(Cost Basis, Salvage Value, Life, Period, 2)

You will find the formula or function-statement in MS Excel only works when using 10% salvage value. Any salvage value higher than 10% and the recovery period will be corrupted or end too soon. This will require an adjustment.

Also, if for example you use a 7 year life and a 10% salvage value a mid-year or half-year convention you will note the cost recovery will extend to the 8th year. AND yes, "conventions" addressing when an asset is placed into service are used in both GAAP and MACRS methods. Further, these conventions are also used when an asset is disposed of as well or when calculating remaining value for determining gain or loss when sold. See section 8.2 for more information.

Mid-Quarter Convention is used if the property was placed in service during the last quarter of the taxable year and total depreciable bases of MACRS calculated property exceeds 40%. If you place property in service between January and September, the first nine months, you must use the half-year convention. Mid-Month Convention means property placed into service after the 1st of any month.

8.1.3   SYD - Sum of Year Digits

Under the SYD method, the depreciation rate percentage for each year is calculated as the number of years in remaining asset life for the same year divided by the sum of remaining asset life every year through the asset's life. As the depreciation rate decreases over time, so does the depreciation charge. The formula used is as follows: =SYD (Cost Basis, Salvage Value, Life, Period)

You will note the SYD depreciation when calculated with an MS Excel function-statement the residual value is not corrupted by 10%, 20%, or 30% salvage value and not adjustment is required for the remaining periods(s).

8.1.4   Units of Production Method

This method is often used for production tooling. For example, if a set of tool steel dies used to cast a mold part is good for 100,000 parts or if the die plates are aluminum and good for up to 10,000 parts.   Then depreciation is based on units of production made during each reporting period.

8.2   MACRS (Modified Accelerated Cost Recovery System) Tables

One of the first differences between the GAAP or "Book Method" when compared to the MACRS or Income Tax Method is with MACRS there is no salvage value. Using the annual percentages for depreciation given in the tables in the IRS 946 Publication, at the end of those recovery schedules the value is zero.

With MACRS calculating annual depreciation is easy. It only requires that you use the percentages used in the IRS tables until the asset value reaches zero.

However, you must also use the tables in Appendix A of the IRS Publication 946 to determine the percentages based on when the asset was placed into service:

- Mid-Month Convention
- Mid-Quarter Convention
- Half Year Convention

When using these required first year conventions you will note the depreciation will change for the year the purchase took place or first period and each year thereafter until the last allowed year of life. These conventions may also cause property with an IRS specified life of 7 years to extend to 8 years before reaching zero. Just go by the IRS specified annual percentages for each convention and asset class stipulated in Appendix B of the IRS Publication 946.

8.3   IRS Reference Publications

Here is a list of IRS publications that provide guidance. Depreciation can get very complicated so always consult with your CPA before publishing or filing statements or tax returns.

IRS Publication 551 - "Basis of Assets"
IRS Publication 946 – "How to Depreciate Property" – includes Section 179 guidance
IRS Publication 544 - "Sales and Other Dispositions of Assets"
IRS Publication 535 - "Business Expenses"

Note: Refer to the appendices in each of these IRS publications for a complete list of publications that deal with asset depreciation and amortization.

8.4   Safe Harbor Limits – Capitalize or Expense

The term "Safe Harbor" when referring to asset depreciation means the cost basis amount specified by the IRS or GASB that is less than an established amount set by the governing body (IRS or GASB) where the asset can be expensed. The limit was $500 and was raised to $2,500 recently for small companies without "Applicable" (audited) Financial Statements. Those with applicable statements may expense assets under $5,000. GASB requires all governmental entities to expense assets less than $5,000 by law. In other words, it's mandatory. For companies the amount established for expensing asset is optional, but in either case it must be spelled out in a written policy and remain constant. Both IRS and GASB rules regarding making changes made to a previously established amount must be followed.

8.5   Bonus & Section 179 Depreciation

The Section 179 deduction and bonus depreciation are two ways to get your entire cost recovery upfront. So what's the difference between Section 179 and bonus depreciation? Section 179 lets business owners deduct a set dollar amount of new business assets, and bonus depreciation lets them deduct a percentage of the cost.

In 2002, President Bush and Congress passed a new accelerated depreciation provision called "bonus depreciation" into law that allowed an immediate 50% deduction. On December 22, 2017 President Trump signed into law, The Tax Cuts and Jobs Act increasing that deduction to 100%. This new rate remains in place from assets placed into service from September 17, 2017 to December 31, 2022. After that the following cost recovery schedule applies:

- 80% for property placed in service after December 31, 2022 and before January 1, 2024.
- 60% for property placed in service after December 31, 2023 and before January 1, 2025.
- 40% for property placed in service after December 31, 2024 and before January1, 2026.
- 20% for property placed in service after December 31, 2025 and before January 1, 2027.

The tax code regarding this new accelerated cost recovery is complicated and applies differently to various asset classes and other qualifications, so again consult with your CPA before filing or publishing financial statements.

8.6   Loss Recovery – calculating loss & insurance reimbursement

Calculating Cost Impairment or loss due to fire, damage due to weather, or other events such as a break down will require you calculate your loss. However, the IRS will not allow a deduction normally, until a sale of the property reserve item is made or it is disposed of. If the property is covered by insurance and a claim is filed and/or paid by the insurance company, the resultant gain or loss much be calculated before filing.

Refer to IRS Publication 551 for Decreases in Cost Basis, adjustments, and allowable write downs. To comply with GAAP for private entities refer to FASB 144. For municipalities and/or government entities refer to GASB 42.

Chapter 9 – Asset Disposition

9.0   Overview

Asset Disposition is where most companies drop the ball. They're pretty good at maintaining depreciation and amortization schedules, but have little or no documented process in place for when an asset is transferred out of service for maintenance, sale, donation, or disposal.

Whether the disposition of an asset is a write-up or a write-down on the books will depend on the remaining Net of Amortization when taken out of service, its GAAP based salvage value, its sale price, and any gain should the "impairment" be covered by insurance. A journal prepared with the remaining Net of Depreciation and/or GAAP based salvage value prior to its disposition should be maintained.

9.1   Property Reserve – Quarantine Area

The best way to quantify assets that have been taken out of service is to complete an Asset Disposition Report for each asset and to store those items in a quarantined area under lock and key until their disposition is processed. A sample ADR is displayed in Appendix (T). There you can see the kind of data is required. In large companies this area of their plant is normally referred to as a Property Reserve. A company can use this area to sell these assets or hold auctions. Key data from ADRs can be exported to Excel or some other database for generate a total current listing.

Of course, once property is removed from use or service it should be taken off the company's depreciation and amortization schedule. As this inventory is sold, donated, or scrapped the resultant gain or loss should be calculated accordingly.

In order to preserve the full value of the asset, a copy of the Property Record should be carefully reviewed to ensure all combination accessories are included with the base asset, along with the User or Service manuals.

If an asset requires either in-house or outside service and must be removed from the factory floor then a shipping memo should be prepared along with any corresponding Work Order. Further, when shipped outside for service the item or its property number should appear on a Shipping Log.

Always include a disclaimer on corresponding documentation that the item being sent to outside contractors for service is being sent "under bailment" which is a legal term that makes the service contractor or auctioneer responsible for its safe keeping until it is returned or sold and payment is delivered.

9.2   Risk Assessment Practices

There are two things it is normally advisable to do when selling or auctioning off assets: (1) to include a disclaimer that your company is selling the item or items "As Is", meaning without any warranty expressed or implied nor is your company liable in any way for damages or injury during its use; and (2) to remove all Property Labels and/or RFID tags upon sale - the concept being, not to be someone's "deep pocket".

9.3   Property Reserve Sales

Some companies contract out sales of assets in property reserve and some sell it directly from the quarantine area where it is warehoused. When sold directly a Bill of Sale should be employed to maintain a record of each sale. A sample Bill of Sale eForm is displayed in Appendix (U). Note the disclaimer warning the buyer that the item is sold "As Is" and that no warranty is either expressed or implied.

9.4   Donations

The advantage of donating spent or used equipment is you can deduct its actual remaining value on your books, meaning the book value and/or the reserve salvage value. Make sure you get a receipt from the organization you are donating the item to – make, model, and serial number as well as the Property No. you originally assigned to it.

9.5   Employing Auctioneers – under bailment

The Appendix (V) is a sample eForm employed for a list of assets consigned to a contractor or auctioneer to repair, sell, or dispose of. You will note the disclaimer at the bottom of that form that makes clear all assets on the list are delivered "under bailment". This is a legal term that makes the consignee responsible for the assets until payment or repair is completed and delivered back to your company. The term "under bailment" also supersedes and bankruptcy proceeding where assets "under bailment" must by law be returned to your company. Note: this disclaimer also includes terms regarding any residual amount set for an auction and that all Bills of Sale must make clear items sold are "As Is" and the company assumes no liability for its use.

9.6   Taxes – on Gain or (Loss)

When presenting proof during an IRS audit you should maintain a file which includes the Property Record and Property Number similar to the one displayed in Appendix (K), Cost Basis Record displayed in Appendix (J), the Asset Disposition Report (ADR) in Appendix (T), and a Bill of Sale similar to the one displayed in Appendix (U) as well as a copy of your Depreciation and Amortization Detail Sheet displaying the book value and salvage value.

If you look at the last section in the ADR you will note how the calculation written into the data filed for Sale Amount, Book Value, Salvage Value, and Claim Proceeds = either a Gain or (Loss).   The tax on any gain is taxable at the regular tax rate.

Chapter 10 – Internal Controls

10.0   Overview – GAAP Internal Controls & Purpose
Internal controls are designed to prevent fraud and clerical errors that may compromise the accuracy of a company's financial statements. Solid internal controls can also reduce losses from theft of company assets and identify underperforming employees. These controls should be implemented by the company before any financial information is given to external auditors, lenders, or investors. It doesn't matter whether you are referring to a company under FASB or a government entity under GASB, the meaning is the same, the internal controls serve the same purpose.

10.1   Basic Principles
There are five primary principles of internal controls:
- Segregation of Duties
- Controlled Access
- Authorization
- GAAP Record Keeping
- Verification

10.1.1   Segregation of Duties
This means separating tasks in such a way as to prevent fraud, but more importantly to create double-check procedures to reduce clerical errors. For example, the person who is tasked to reconcile bank statements should not also receive payments from customers or make bank deposits; nor, would you want the same person who does purchasing to write checks to vendors. This takes a careful analysis. It requires a signature of the employee performing the task and a supervisor or department head to approve the work product.

10.1.2   Controlled Access
This includes installing both physical and software controls to ensure only authorized employees have access to assets, files, and/or electronic records. Also, if keypads, biometric, RFID locks, or passwords are employed to gain access, a record of those "keys" should be maintained at all times in a secure file. Typically, the IT department head is responsible for such security with respect to electronic records and keypad or biometric locks, as well as the responsibility to create or revise form templates. This includes the task of generating batch recordsets, establishing assess levels for each batch and granting privilege to each user in the process routing schedule, as well as file storage and archival – usually in accordance with a documented convention for field, file, and folder naming and location.

In addition to controlled access, allowing everyone in the organization to view various records can ensure a second set of eyes on operations. For example, granting Read-Only access of Purchase Orders and Property Records can help others spot discrepancies or items that never made it through to placement. However, there should always be a purpose for granting such rights.

All of the above is typically controlled by IT only, but subject to signature approval of a Compliance Officer or CEO. Changes to the eform template are normally done on an IT work station only. With most systems there are also various levels of access and privileges granted on a case by case basis depending on the task assignment. For example, most computer programs used for operations will have various levels of rights granted: (1), the right to change passwords; (2) the right to open and view only; and (3), the right to open and make data entries. The figure below displays this feature in Formdocs*:

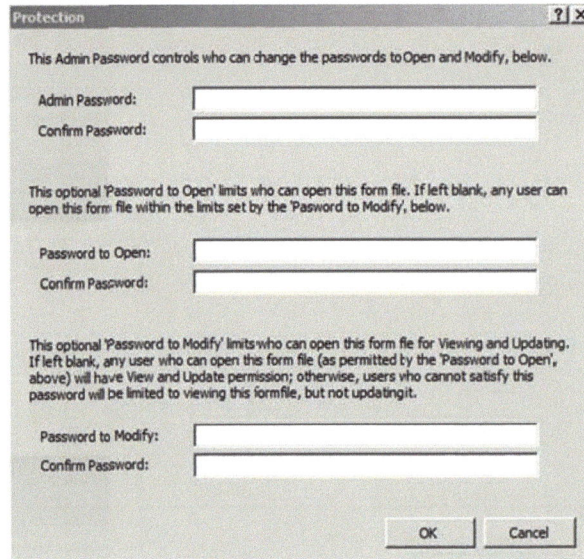

Figure 10.1

10.1.3 Authorization

If a business does not already have one, it should draft and maintain a procedure for all transactions, including a list of employees with the authority to approve each type of transaction. This includes setting limits for each transaction where approvals must first be obtained from supervisors or department heads. Most systems generate a routing map and elaborate controls are embedded in the program to control each task in this manner. The borders around each data field can also be color coded for data entry assignments.

Forms that record events, in addition have provision for dual signatures to enforce segregation of duties, each e-signature should also lock specific data fields once data is entered into a data field to prevent unauthorized changes. The figure below displays that feature in Formdocs*

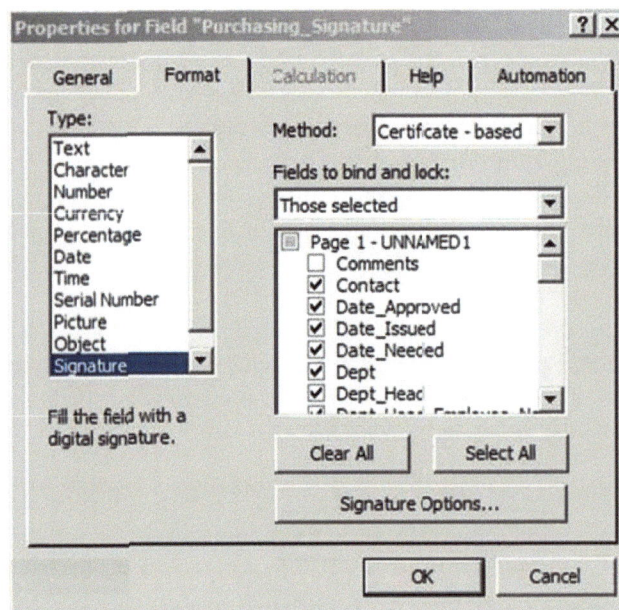

Figure 10.2

Although, every electronic record system is different when you purchase Filler licenses from Formdocs* Authorization is built into their Workflow Routing features as displayed below:

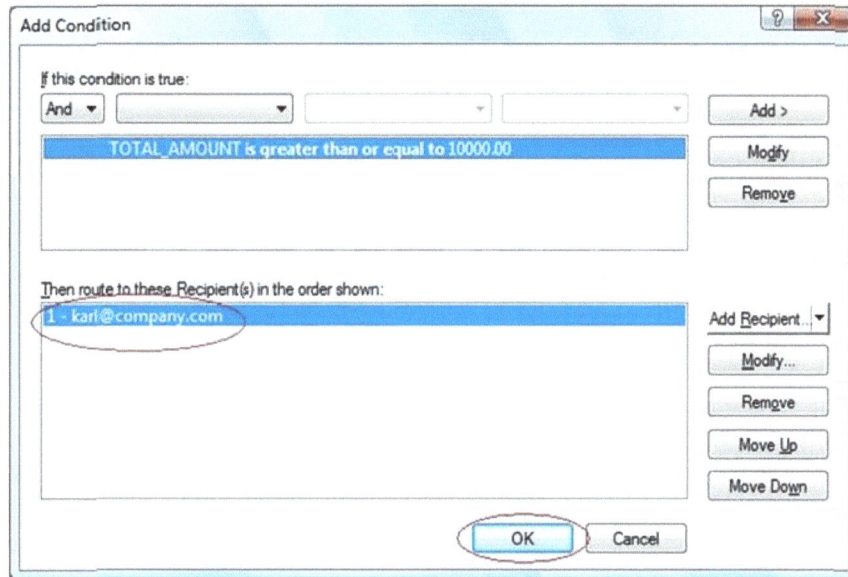

Figure 10.3

This feature includes a Routing Slip with instructions as well as conditions or limitations for each task in the routing process from user to user, including dictating required signatures when dollar amounts are exceeded. This is usually illustrated in a Routing Map or Flow Chart by job title, and listing the various functions and records associated with each task in the processing path.

10.1.4 GAAP Record Keeping
All financial statements should be backed up by general ledger or related journals. Notes should be maintained to any changes in GL accounts. Fraud or accidental errors can be avoided by using standardized forms for all financial transactions. These forms or recordsets should be supported and controlled with a documented Document Control Record (DCR) system that not only list all Data Collection records, but also maintain a record of any revisions to those recordsets. There should be a schema or convention for numbering each form template. That form number is typically at the bottom of the form and includes the form number, Rev Code, and the date. A listing of all forms the business uses should also be maintained and update as revisions are made in a Volume III OMS manual for data collection records. We used our Org Chart and assigned prefixes for records used by each department within the business. To comply with GAAP all eforms should be sequentially numbered with a seed and ending serial number for each FYE or reporting period (i.e. like purchase orders or invoices) to identify missing forms or records.

10.1.5 Verification
Verification requires that someone be given the task of reviewing the general ledger accounts for accuracy. More important this should be someone that has no hand in preparing the journals, or general ledger. For example, the AR Clerk would not be the one to reconcile the Cash Receipts and Sales Journal, nor would the Purchasing Agent be the same person as the AP Clerk who writes checks. The person to oversee all reconciliations or the General Ledger is typically a Chief Compliance Officer or the Finance Director as well as to perform internal audits prior to presentment.   In addition to other tasks, while performing internal audits an eye should be kept on relevant financial metrics to find areas experiencing efficiency problems.

10.2 Implementing Internal Controls

Businesses with fewer than 100 employees account for the highest percentage of fraud instances and higher median loss than their larger counterparts, as reported by the Association of Certified Fraud Examiners (ACFE). So, the sooner a company installs internal controls the better off it will be.

Of course, every business should start with a carefully drafted business plan in hand that includes a description of its business model; meaning, how it will provide its product or service and get paid doing so. Hopefully, that plan will include a proforma income and related cash flow study along with gap analysis and have its applied unit cost detailed. Below the contribution line on the P&L it should also have some idea of CAC (Customer Acquisition Cost). A repeat accessory associated with the use of the lead-in base product will usually go a long way to improve such cost, usually reported as a percentage of sales revenue. Startups will find their CAC to be higher and should taper as the business matures. If not, it has a problem. If you're providing a service adding a subscription component can serve the same propose.

Although, it may be referenced in a Business Plan, an Operation Manual is usually drafted as a separate document. Today they refer to this manual as a QMS (Quality Management System). This is a three part manual that includes: (1) policies; (2) directives (procedures); and (3), a list and samples of data collection records. Like a Business Plan this document is often revised as the company grows. The internationally recognized standard most businesses comply with is ISO 9001. If you're a small job shop or service firm you may fall under ISO 9002. Various industries have their own particular standard based on ISO 9001. For example, medical device manufacturers are required by the FDA to comply with ISO 13485 as well as FDA QSR (Quality System Regulations). Businesses would also do well to adhere to various process standards like ISO 55000 in the case of Asset Management Systems.

10.2.1 Structuring Operations vs Size

Whether you're a small business with just several employees or a larger one, drafting an operations manual should start with an Org Chart. Once drafted and task assignments are indicated for each employee as well as the managers, you'll need to draft job descriptions, along with the skill sets or certifications to perform those tasks. Also where finances are involved a plan for segregation of duties will be needed. In any business there are usually several processes that need to be completed to make the business function. Process routing maps should be drafted to reflect task assignments in prerequisite order of completion. This should be reflected in the QMS manual, including corresponding policies, procedures, and a list of data collection records. Samples of various e-form templates are displayed in the Appendix, mainly for procurement and asset management.

10.2.2 Facility Design

If you're operating as a virtual corporation or business by sub-contracting or outsourcing functional tasks via licensing agreements, then facility design may not be a big concern. For most businesses, whether they are providing a product or a service require facility design to conduct business. For example, if you're purchasing material, supplies, and equipment you will require an adequate receiving dock. If you're storing inventory items you will require an inventory stores area large enough to satisfy operations until your lease expires. Your business model will dictate all other parts of your operating facility. Today it would be difficult to operate without at least one computer workstation at each task based site. This will usually require a LAN server, a cloud account, and file backup. Refer to the Network System drawing in section 4.2.

10.2.3 Cost Projections

Obviously, small businesses can't just build out their staff in each department to some ideal level to fully satisfy *Segregation of Duties*. The other four primary GAAP based internal controls are a bid easier to satisfy without adding more bodies. However, cost is a factor in any operating plan. So to satisfy *Segregation of Duties* some careful thought will be required. Refer to section 10.3.4 for some ideas.

10.2.4 Employee Training to Ensure Sustainability

It may not be practical to document personnel training programs when a small business is starting out, but at some point documented training and personnel certification programs will be required to ensure your business can sustain its operations as employees come and go, as well as satisfy compliance standards. At first, the owner or manager may have to conduct such training and certification programs themselves. Refer to Appendix W for ideas on how to make personnel training go easier.

10.2.5 Technology and Software Basic to Internal Controls

In additional to employing barcoded property labels, some businesses will use RFID tagging to monitor the movement of assets in and out of their facility by installing antennas at each exit or port within their facility and employ software to monitor those events. To be effective, a combination of video surveillance and RFID technology is often used. The recordings are stored to the Cloud for follow-up viewing or monitored real time by a security force in larger businesses.

If you're a small business we recommend you install a relational database e-form record system to both record data that can be exported from batch recordsets to reports and used to autofill data to new records, to prevent manual manipulation of static data. There are a number of relational database e-form systems, but we use Formdocs*, a Windows based replacement for FormFlow* which was popular during the 1990's until about 2006. Formdocs* is ODBC compliant. With this software two or more e-signatures can be added to a record to satisfy Segregation of Duties as well as lock specific field data with those signatures.

The appendix includes various examples of e-forms as well as corresponding reports. Appendices N, O, P, and Q demonstrates how data from e-form recordsets can be used to generate reports and also to autofill data to both prevent data from being changed by unauthorized employees and to pull data into new records from up-to-date database records or Excel* spreadsheets to reduce fill time and to ensure consistency.

With a system like this in place a small or large company can employ the *Read-Only* privilege to give access to any number of employees in the organization to ensure a second-set of eyes are on all transactions.

10.3 Forensic Accounting – Exposing Fraud

There are a number of professional associations with membership listings of forensic accountants:
- Institute of Certified Forensic Accountants
- National Association of Forensic Accountants
- Association of Certified Fraud Examiners
- American Board of Forensic Accounting
- American Institute of CPAs

Of course, before a forensic accountant can come in to scrutinize your books for misappropriation of funds or inspect records for missing assets, your business first has to have records in place to perform such an audit. This is one of the primary principles of GAAP based internal controls – GAAP based records. A formal retention policy can work against discovery of fraud or embezzlement when years old. In other words, without records finding wrong doing is much harder. This is especially important since Statute of Limitation laws in most states also state that period begins from the date of discovery. For example, in Washington State the statute reads as follows:

RCW 4.16.080(6)
Actions limited to three years. However, the law states: "...regardless of lapse of time or existing statute of limitation, or the bar thereof, even though complete, shall exist and be enforceable for three years after discovery by aggrieved party of the act or acts from which such liability has arisen or shall arise."

Also, in most cases misappropriation is not discovered on average until well beyond (3) years. This means you could be scrutinizing records going back over (20) years or more, depending on the date of discovery. Hence, at the very least, it's wise to keep purchase orders, vendor invoices, and packing lists going back in digital form for whatever number of years lapsed since your last examination, even if you have to scan hardcopy documents received from vendors daily as a routine practice.

Federal law requires banks keep records for checking and savings accounts for (5) five years. You may want to check with your bank to see what their retention policy is and what is involved to obtain those records when required. This is also a good reason to keep bank statements, journals, and ledgers going back (20) years or more, especially if you are a government entity. You may want to inspect Pay-to-the-Order-of stamps on the back side of cancelled checks each month as they are received from the bank. Don't forget to review vendors routinely for authenticity and check for any payments made to unapproved vendors.

Of course, when you find fraud, depending on the amount taken you will have to make the decision to prosecute or not. Refer to Chapter (14) titled, "Dealing with Bad Actors".

10.3.1 Whistleblower Act
Did you know that Whistleblowers are not only protected by law from dismissal or retaliation, but they can be entitled to a portion of the misappropriated funds as well. For example, in Washington State, public employee Whistleblower awards in a successful action may receive an award of between 15% and 25% percent if the state Attorney General intervenes and proceeds with the action. The laws for Whistleblowers in the private sector are different. In fact, the law varies between states, federal agencies, and the private sector. We recommend you seek legal advice before taking any action, but if your evidence of wrongdoing is solid, it should not be hard to find a law firm to take on anyone who comes at you for whatever reason. However, be forewarned, Whistleblowers as a general rule do not always fare well. See the case study below.

10.3.2 Case Studies
In Edmonds, Washington an HR Director was fired when she discovered the interim Mayor was paying his lady friend for hours never worked. After the next Mayor was elected, the HR Director was put back on temporarily, but the new Mayor later reported to her that the city council had decided to eliminate her position, as if that would fly. She filed suit and the City ended up paying her over a $1million in damages. It was a long battle, but she won. AND yes, if you're whistleblowing on a department head or elected official in a government entity that entity and their attorney will often circle the wagons and attempt to discredit you or find a way to let you go. It's their job to protect the city from liability, but in this case a big mistake, as this City discovered the hard way. Also, in this case the State Auditor conducted an audit to confirm the wrong doing prior to this woman's court case. In addition, during the audit, the State Auditors found other employees were also paid without working the hours and that the payroll clerk, as a matter of practice was writing checks when time sheets were missing department head or a supervisor's signature, without confirming hours were actually worked - a total lack of *Segregation of Duties*. From all indications, this practice was in place long before the interim Mayor showed up.

The Finance Director of the Pierce County Housing Authority in Tacoma Washington admitted in court that she misappropriated nearly $7million. It was the largest public fraud on record in Washington State as of 2019. The fraud, according to the State Auditor's Report was perpetrated over a period of four years from 2016 to 2019. This included phony vendors, phony invoices, and payments directed to private bank accounts. The reports claimed others in the agency were involved via payoffs. Your tax dollars at work.

The Finance Director of SERS (Snohomish Emergency Radio System) in Washington State misappropriated nearly $200,000 before he was caught. According to the news accounts, he later took his own life. SERS was reportedly reimbursed by their Fidelity Bonding Agency.

This is just three cases in Western Washington alone and there are others so you can imagine how many there are nationwide, even more in private industry. None of these government entities took *Segregation of Duties* or other internal controls seriously. If so, these cases may not have taken place.

According to a study done by Hiscox, the average loss for cases that continued for five years or more was $2.2 million, and for cases lasting 10 years or more, the average loss was $5.4 million. This report can be viewed in its entirety at https://www.hiscox.com/documents/2018-Hiscox-Embezzlement-Study.pdf Of course the amounts will depend on the size of company in any sample.

However, as you can see the longer it takes to discover the fraud the amount embezzled increases accordingly. This study also discovered that in 79% of the fraud cases involved, on average three employees were working in concert. My research always showed only one lone wolf in most cases. However, if true this may fly in the face of Segregation of Duties, but fraud can still be detected. In a small business, the CEO can inspect the books or in larger businesses consultants can be hired from outside the business to detect misappropriation regardless whether perpetrated by a lone wolf or by a collaborative effort.

10.3.3 Impediments to Corrective Action
In private industry the absence of internal controls is typically due to weak or overworked management which relies on staff to watch over transactions. Obviously, staff should never be allowed to police itself.

In government entities, the absence of internal controls is usually due to the fact that Mayors or other officials lack operations experience entirely. They too rely on staff and staff typically has no desire to restructure their procedures or change anything they have been doing. Often their staff is poorly trained.

When dealing with government entities, often elected officials will deny access and even mislead the public to protect the perception all is well. Anything contrary to that perception is a negative reflection on them and their chance for re-election. Even after government state auditors discover an absence of internal controls citizens who understand these audit reports and voice concerns are often dismissed or ignored. It's just easier for all other elected officials to just go along to get along. Further, you will find that there is no process in place to ensure corrective action was ever put in place in a sustainable manner and city officials are reluctant to provide competent proof of corrective action after adverse findings are reported.

Regardless, for all these reasons or more bad actors can go undetected for years and when embezzlement is finally uncovered the amounts can be so large the only hope to recover the misappropriated funds is from the entity's fidelity bonding agency, if they have one. Of course, depending on the amount it almost always results in an increase in the entity's experience rate and insurance premiums or perhaps results in that entity being dropped immediately thereafter by their bonding agency.

In the end, it's the CEO who must take responsibility for implementing internal controls and see to it internal audits are performed before financials are presented. If he or she does not know how to do this, then it's up to them to commission a contracting agency to perform such internal audits or hire a Chief Compliance Officer with the necessary skill sets to ensure operations and all journals are properly reconciled and the General Ledger is properly maintained and all accounts are in balance at each FYE.

10.3.4 Examination
First, let no one know you're looking. If you're a small company you can perform a routine inspection yourself or hire an agency to do it. The best time to examine records is on the weekend when employees are not in the office. Although, a good defense against embezzlement is a QMS (Quality Management System) Manual with documented policies, procedures with GAAP internal controls built-in, and a list of data collection records, routine inspection is the best defense.

Further, the lack of internal controls is often never remedied in a permanent way. The main reason for this is that in order to ensure sustainability as department heads and employees come and go over time, without documented training and certification programs in place, adverse findings or citations tend to ebb and flow.

As stated in Chapter (1) most fraud takes place in the front of any Asset Management System, or during the procurement process, usually due to the absence of Segregation of Duties; in other words, separating purchasing from receiving, and again from accounts payable as well as requiring two signatures during each step in the procurement process. Theft of tangible assets takes place due to the absence of tagging and tracking assets either before they are put into service or after. This includes a method of tracking the disposition of assets all the way to their end-of-life and disposal or sale.

One of the most common schemes used by bad actors is to create phony vendors and vendor invoices, then divert funds to an address they control. Having a policy and procedure in place to require more than one signature to approve the use of vendors will go a long way to foil this scheme.

Also, to ensure that goods are actually received for each purchase recorded is to maintain a **Daily Receiving Log by Receiving Date, Pack List number, reference PO, and carrier tracking number**. The log should include an indication when asset items are included. That procedure should require inspection of goods against the pack list and purchase order. All asset items should be tagged with a unique property number before it is transferred or placed into service, and recorded in a Property Record by make, model, and serial number as well as other data readily available during receiving such as vendor name, Pack List number, and reference PO. Vendor payment should be preceded by a process whereby the Pack List is matched with the Vendor Invoices and the reference PO. Finally, a list of AP payments should be delivered to the finance manager for approval prior to release.

Beyond the fraud committed within the Asset Management System, it can also take place in payroll and in managing receipts from sales when segregation of duties are absent or when two or more signatures are not required; for example, not requiring supervisor signatures on all time sheets, or requiring a manager's signature when cutting and/or releasing payroll checks. Another example is not separating the collection of cash receipts from the employee making deposits. Maintaining a Cash Receipts & Sales Journal to reconcile serialized invoices and cash receipts with check register deposits can go a long way to spot missing funds in real time. A careful review of all of the above should be performed routinely to spot anomalies. The more sophisticated the perpetrator, the harder these anomalies will be to spot.

10.4 Sarbanes-Oxley Act (SOX) - for Investors & Corporate Officers
The SOX Act was passed by the federal government to protect investors from the lack of reliable financial information and/or operations void of internal controls.

Since its enactment in 2002, the Sarbanes-Oxley Act ("SOX") has been widely perceived to regulate only publically held companies. That perception is not, nor has it ever been correct. There are some provisions of SOX that expressly apply to privately held companies. In addition, lenders, investors, and potential business partners consider SOX corporate governance requirements to establish "best practices" for both public and private companies. Finally, failure to comply with fundamental SOX requirements can impair a potential public offering or a sale to a public company. It can also potentially give investors a means to pierce the corporate vale and come directly at corporate officers or general partners in the absence of internal controls and/or reliable financial information as well as the required written reports to comply with SOX.

However, local municipalities are exempt from SOX. Instead investors of municipal bonds rely on rating services, like Moody's for Fitch. So, does that mean when a city is given an AAA bond rating its books are clean and GAAP based internal controls are in place? – not really. For example, when comparing cities with AAA bond ratings to their State Audit Reports, you may find a city's books are out of balance by an amount that far exceeds what in the accounting world is considered "material" before the auditors show up; in some cases, by 5% or even by more than 10%. In fact, account errors can include unfunded pension obligations or the lack of liability reserves for such obligations.

So, just how reliable are these private rating services and what are the ratings based on? You can research this yourself, but these ratings have more to do with income demographics and the "reported" debt level a city has at the time the rating is given, not how well they manage their books.

The next question an investor should ask is just what enforcement mechanisms exist to protect investors of Muni Bonds? Answer - none! For example, in Washington State as the SAO will attest they can only audit, discover deficiencies, and recommend. The only enforcement option they have is to contract with the State Police or other law enforcement entity to begin a criminal investigation, but that's after the fact or only after funds have been misappropriated. Typically, that action only begins when a Whistleblower comes forward.

The State's Sunshine Laws or Public Records Act ("PRA") offer some insight into what's really going on or whether or not a municipality, county, or local governmental agency is complying with GAAP or GASB regulations, but does little good if a lack of enforcement exist.

For example, in the State of Washington the statue RCW 43.09.230 requires that all municipalities must submit financial statements by May 30 for the preceding FYE. The law states this date is mandatory with no exceptions. A standard Form must accompany that submission that certificates those financial statements are accurate upon submission. So, what happens if the submission is late and certified by the Finance Director and Mayor as accurate and found later to be in error by as much as 15%. Are there any fines for late submissions or any repercussions for submitting inaccurate statements?

Fact is, you would be hard pressed to find any enforcement cases or even a public rebuke of Finance Directors or officials other than the State Auditor's published Audit Report detailing those adverse findings.

It might shock you to know many cities have AAA bond ratings and their State Auditors preface each FYE audit report with the following statement: ***"The City's internal controls over accounting and financial preparation were not adequate to ensure accurate financial reporting."*** This can go on for years without corrective action. So, is it any wonder how easy it is for a bad actor to operate under the radar for years before someone wakes up. Cost over runs on capital improvement projects are another area of concern. Many cities operate without terms governing Change Orders Pricing in their boilerplate agreement with contractors and worse, often these contracts are let without following state bidding guidelines.

Of course, more often than not few stakeholders ever bother to look at these Audit Reports or make a PRA request for copies of Management Letters sent to city Mayors regarding deficiencies in GAAP based internal controls. So, if you're an investor in Muni Bonds it's buyer beware or perhaps do your own research in addition to relying on a rating service.

Further, there is nothing preventing the rating service from changing it's rating on a dime – like it did when Orange County CA suddenly filed for bankruptcy some years ago or after news of "material" misstatements were made public.

Of course, for public or private corporations Muni Bonds only become an issue when investing in them, holding them on your balance sheet, or operating in a municipality that is poorly managed.

Chapter 11 – Securing Assets in Place & in Storage

11.0 Overview
When I started my manufacturing many years ago I had to learn the hard way that if you expect employees to be as honest as you, you're in for a sad awaking. I started my company from very humble beginnings. At first we just let our assemblers keep their assigned tools on top of their respective assembly benches. When that didn't work, we went out and purchased small tool boxes with paddle locks and keys – about 40 of them as I recall. We stocked them with various hand tools. We affixed numbered property labels to each box and maintained a list of tools in each box. At first employees started to lose their assigned keys, then by the year of the year, after taking an inventory of these tool boxes, we found more than half of them went missing.

We went from that approach to finally securing workstation tools in locked drawers attached to the underside of workstation benches. After you're in business for twenty years, you tend to build a learning curve. Of course, this was before the days of keypads or biometric locks. We also found ourselves embroiled in employee related law suits when we caught them stealing and tried to hold them responsible for lost assets assigned to them. Refer to section 14.3 for more information on accountability issues.

11.1 Stationary Assets
We didn't have a lot of incidents of theft with Stationary Assets except, even with an auto-dialer alarm system in place we came in one morning to find a new XT computer missing. You can make it harder by using tethered cables, etc. but that doesn't always stop them. Today, computers come with a variety of tracking methods. You can also use services like Lojack* or track IP addresses by using Apps like Gmail or Dropbox. Of course, good luck in getting some local police departments to go out the find it even after you have pinpointed its location. If they are willing to go out and arrest the perpetrators just make sure you have the *Property Record* and a copy of the *Invoice*, unless of course they were dumb enough to leave the *Property-of* label on the asset in question. In addition to all of the above the best defense is to have labels with serialize UHF RFID tags and a system to alert you when assets are taken out of the facility.

11.2 Mobile Assets
Securing mobile assets are even more difficult. We already covered in Chapter 6 how various assets are managed and tracked from a Tool Crib, Departmental Storage Lockers, or locked workstation drawers. Now the next consideration is which type of lock is the most appropriate in each case.

11.3 Departmental Storage Lockers
As we made clear in Chapter 6 some assets used by various departments within your company or organization are best kept locked within their respective areas of frequent use. We recommend that access to these cabinets be restricted to department heads only. We could recommend bio-metric locks, but access may be required on some days when that department head is absent, so access may have to made by executive level management. We found the best type of lock for such cabinets is via keypad entry.

11.4 HR Department Assets
The storage cabinet in the HR department supports a *Chain of Custody* process that could affect all other access security and employee accountability, so a *Log* of asset consignments upon hiring and returns during the Exit Interview are critical. A keypad lock should be sufficient and again the only other person authorized to gain access to this cabinet should be the HR Director's or executive manager. Each release or return requires additional paperwork to be filed in the employee's jacket – maintained by the HR Director.

11.5   Tool Crib

A *Tool Crib* should be a cage off area with a Dutch style door where assets are released to only employees authorized to check them out. Refer to Appendix R to view an example of a date/time stamped record used to record all releases and returns of assets normally stored inside the *Tool Crib*. Any employee making a request to check out an asset must have their employee badge which includes their photo, department, and employee number or badge number. Some companies use suffix privacy codes (or pin number) that each employee must know to prevent use of counterfeit badges. Obviously, this is going to be a bigger issue in larger companies or organizations. Also to make sure that assets are being released to the right employee a copy of the *Work Order* (*WO*) should be routed to the Tool Crib and that *WO* number should be referenced on each release record. The *WO* should reference the employee assigned the task.

11.6   Employee Controlled Storage – Workstation Drawers

As we mentioned lost keys seem to be a more frequent occurrence as you move down through the ranks within your company or organization. Every time a key goes missing, that lock is no longer secure so not only a new key must be made, but new locks and the cost of installation is also required. Also, when assets consigned to employees on the floor go missing it's too easy for the employee to claim innocence. The best way to avoid that is to use bio-metric locks on all workstation drawers.

Employees are required to notify their supervisor as soon as an asset goes missing and to put their tools back into the locked drawer at the end of their shift. If you have multiple shifts and more than one employee must have access to a workstation drawer then it is up to employees to check their tool list before each shift and notify their supervisor of missing or damaged tools or supply items. An inventory of tools for that workstation drawer should be included within each drawer. We used plasticized cards.

11.7   Types of Locking Devices & Monitoring Issues

To recap, we advise against using keys whenever possible. They're just too hard and costly to manage as well as hold anyone accountable for loss. We like coded keypads for larger storage cabinets and bio-metric locks for personal workstation drawers. They're both easily reset when employee turnover takes place.

Of course, Video, RFID, and GPS locating systems are great, but the issue is whether or not you can afford to have a full time *Security Officer* to monitor this real time activity. Most Video cameras are motion activated like RFID tag systems and incidents can be stored for later viewing. Of course, at best you may not realize an asset was taken out of the facility until the next time you check. Even with a *Security Officer* there are strict legal limits when confronting a person expected of removing assets, not to mention the safety issues for the *Security Officer* as well. All of this requires careful consideration and terms spelling out those restrictions in *Employment Agreements* and training to avoid liability. Insurance premiums are also bound to increase.

11.8   Vehicle Secure Storage

This, of course, will depend on the size of your company or organization. If you're a smaller company and issue vehicles to only key executives then most likely you are going to allow them to go back and forth to work with that vehicle. However, just don't forget to work out insurance, tax, and liability issues when used for work or home. These terms should be reflected in *Employment Agreements*.

If you're a larger organization and have a secured lot where company vehicles are stored and assignments are managed, then at the very least you should have GPS and whatever *Telematics* software that works for you as well as a log of assignments and returns. RFID can be used in addition to GPS tracking to date/time stamp vehicles as they come and go from the lot. Of course, *Telematics* systems are available to track mileage/gas usage and map routes as well as other logistics depending on the needs of your business.

Chapter 12 – Security

12.0 Overview – recognized compliance standards

A written plan for security as it relates to your facilities and your information technology systems is important if you expect to protect both your physical assets and data. There are a number of compliance standards that can work together, especially aimed at security with respect to Asset Management:

ISO 41001 - Facility management
ISO 55001 - Asset Management Systems
ISO 27001 - Information security management systems
DoD 5220.22-M - National Industrial Security Program - Operating Manual

ISO 41001-Facility Management system requirements: This standard is relatively new and covers all aspects of facility management but is written in general terms.   It references personnel safety, facilities, secure areas, physical assets, and information systems.

ISO 55001-Asset Management: This standard is the gold standard when it comes to Asset Management Systems. This standard and ISO 41001 are promoted as complementing each other.

ISO/IEC 27001:2013-Information technology-Security techniques -*"Information security management systems requirements"* and ISO/IEC 27002:2013 Information technology-Security techniques – *"Code of practice for information security management"*: These standards include best practices for information security controls for those charged with Information Security Management Systems (ISMS) or information security.

The way things are moving so quickly the question many are asking is whether or not certification is worth it. An ISO 27001 certification requires a sizable commitment in requires professionals to administer the compliance standard. A more practical approach may be to make sure you have adequate defenses installed such as anti-virus protection and that your IT operations are under control - especially with respect to *Policies* and *Directives* as well as controlled access. Beyond that you may want to pay close attention to section (12.7). If your company or organization requires third party certification or audits, then ISO 27001 certification may be required.   In the end it's a decision only you can make.

DOD Standard 5220.22-M - titled, "National Industrial Security Program - Operating Manual" (NISPOM). This is a good general guide on facilities security including adopting policy and procedures for personnel, training, and safe guarding assets and files.

ITAR is an acronym defined as "International Traffic in Arms Regulations". Contractors engaged in any way with design or production of arms must be compliant with ITAR regulations. This includes security provisions related to materials covered by the Invention Secrecy Act or any information thereof. No one entity can certify compliance. Instead you register with the Directorate of Defense Trade Controls (DDTC) to get approval to import and export products, data, and services covered by those ITAR regulations.

In fact, to bid on certain DOD contracts in the future you may be required to comply with Cybersecurity Maturity Model Certification (CMMC) which is currently scheduled to go into effect in 2026. Unfortunately, hacking of our industrial and defense secrets have become rampant, not only for profit but also by foreign powers. These files are considered intangible assets and usually are the most valuable assets a company possesses or holds in trust, other than its human capital.

12.1   Security Starts with Good People
It should go without saying; this rule especially applies to those charged with maintaining your company's security. Depending on the size of your business this function may be incorporated with the functions performed by a facilities manager. In larger firms security personnel usually come with prior qualifications in the field as well as professional certifications, many with technical skill sets as well. Refer to section (14.1) titled, "Vetting Candidates for Employment" and section (14.1.4) titled, "Background Checks".

12.2   Written Plan for Security
In addition to policy and personnel rules outlined in Employee Handbooks and various Employment Agreements, a documented plan is required for all aspects of security as well. This may or may not be incorporated into your documented plan for Risk Assessment.

12.3   Controlled Ingress & Egress
Unless it's an office building, most factories or processing plants have at least two ingress and egress portals, plus one or two for shipping and receiving. This includes one for office workers and customers and another for factory workers. A time card or RFID based recording device is typically located at the single ingress/egress point. Most companies require Employee ID Badges that are either barcoded or have an embedded RFID tag or both. Barcodes are commonly used to consign materials and tools by WO. Some companies use RTLS (Real Time Locating System) software to track the whereabouts of employees in real time using Employee ID Badges, same as the location or movement of tagged assets. You may be required by local fire codes to have additional exits and those doors are typically one way – out only.

Most companies have at least video surveillance at each ingress and egress portal as well as near each fire exit to prevent unauthorized entry or "assisted unauthorized entry". To conserve file storage space often such cameras are motion activated. If set up to be monitored by either a facilities manager or security officer then unauthorized use can be detected in real time; otherwise if recorded only, companies will normally install alarms or buzzers at all fire exits to discourage non-emergency use. The use of cloud storage is growing in popularity in order not to limit date and time based recordings.

12.3.1   Building Perimeter
Surveillance of parking areas and the perimeter around the outside of your facility is highly advisable. This will ensure unauthorized access to wiring or service panels as well as prevent the covert installation of devices meant to foil (jam), evade, or gain access to computer systems and files via RF repeaters, etc.

If your facility is only part of an industrial park the park managers may provide a surveillance service for all their building tenants. Large construction firms, for example, will not only fence off a building site for security reasons or to comply with local building authorities for public safety, but may also contract for surveillance services by security firms with remote 24/7 monitoring capabilities. In fact, insurance carriers may insist on it. If trucks or other heavy equipment are stored on the site, GPS tracking devices are typically installed and concealed in hard to find places.

12.3.2   High Security Internal Areas
There may be various areas within your company or organization that will require heightened levels of security such as server rooms, R&D labs, security stations, etc. Those areas may require the use of smart or one-way glass or even faraday shielding. Of course there are many EMI materials available, including EMI paint as well as EMI stripping for doors. The use of RFID readers at each of these entrances can also record who goes in and out date/time stamp that personnel movement.

12.4   Protocols for Employees & Outsiders

Security systems alone will not protect a company from IP theft or loss of data. It will also require a carefully designed and written plan to address the human element. This includes both employees and all those from the outside, especially vendors - "loose lips sink ships". In addition to policies in Employee Handbooks and Employment Agreements it will require documented training programs.

12.4.1   Employee/Visitor Badges & Logs – RFID Tracking

If your company is going to have any kind of security at all, the use of Employee and Visitor Badges are required as well as a visitor log. Today those badges may include embedded RFID tags in order to track the location of employees and visitors as they move through your facility. This will require RFID readers and antennas strategically located throughout the building and RTLS software. If you already have RTLS for asset management you can easily use it for personnel management as well. Of course, this is in addition to any video surveillance your company has in place.

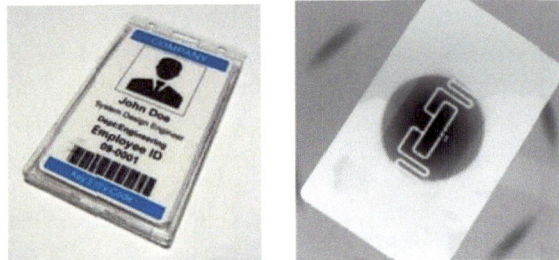

Figure 12.1

Note: When you combine a video surveillance system with RFID tracking and you tag both personnel and assets, a NOX system can record employees moving in and out of your facility with assets, whether authorized or unauthorized.

12.4.2   Protocols – Designated Escorts

No matter how much hardware and software you have in place for plant security, no outsider should be allowed to enter your company facility without a designated escort. There should also be policies in place to limit outsiders or even certain employees from entering sensitive areas within the facility. In fact, although you may want to show outsiders production or other areas in your facility out of pride or whatever reason, it's advisable instead to bring visitors directly into a conference room and limit their view of operations unless it is absolutely necessary.

For example, we used to entertain a sales rep from a key vendor. I noticed he always asked questions regarding our production output. Later I found out at a tradeshow he was using that information to ingratiate himself with our competitor who was a much larger customer.

We had another case of a sales rep who knew well and good we had a gate keeper system in our front office area, but wanted to avoid that so he'd slipped into our facility from our receiving area when the bay door was left wide open on a warm day. We found him wandering into sensitive areas and had him escorted off the premises. We called his employer and told them what had happened and informed them we could no longer allow anyone from their company in our facility.

However, more importantly this incident required us to retrain all those employees who worked in the vicinity of our shipping and receiving docks as to what the ground rules were for outsiders.

12.5 Asset Tracking Methods

We've already covered the use of Property Labels and Tracking Methods in chapters (5) and (6) as well as data collection in chapter (3). The Appendix in this book includes many examples of electronic forms or eForms used in Asset Management. We are covered the various considerations for both stationary and mobile assets in chapter (11). In summary we should discuss the practicality of various methods.

The Asset Tracking Method you employ will depend on the nature of your company, its operations, and the type of assets you manage. For example, where hospitals employ a lot of equipment on wheels, a RTLS (Real Time Locating System) makes sense. However, some companies use RFID tags to only detect movement when going through egress portals or read tagged assets by handheld readers when audited.

12.5.1 Barcode Labels

We covered various barcode symbologies in chapter (5). Basically,1D symbologies can only store one short line of characters, like a Property No. whereas 2D symbologies can store multiple lines of data.

Whether you need a 2D barcode when using, for example, a combination RFID tag which also stores multiple lines of data capable of being read with the proper scanner is a decision you will need to make. Your decision may be related to how data you read on your handheld device gets deposited into your electronic records. Also, remember a barcode with Property No. will assist the authorities who may not have a RFID reader. This is why we recommend combination barcode and embedded RFID tag labels.

12.5.2 NFC & UHF RFID Tags

In chapter (5) in section (5.5) we covered the various types of RFID tags and how some are used for Point of Sale and others for auditing or tracking inventory from a distance. Although, section (5.5) covers a variety of RFID tags, the most popular are NFC (Near Field Communication) and UHF (Ultra High Frequency) tags. NFC tags have only a range of a few cm and UHF tags can be read from much greater distances.

It's the UHF RFID tags that are widely used for security and for auditing inventory. They are passive and in most cases will continue to work well beyond the life of most equipment. They also have the capability to be read from up to 50 feet away with the right antenna and RFID reader. However, UHF RFID tags are typically larger, about 3 inches long and at least 0.75 inches high. Types are available for plastic and metal surfaces or both and are adhesive backed. Distance read depends on antenna gain. See section (12.5.4).

12.5.3 Handheld RFID Readers

In chapter (6) in Figures (6.5) and (6.6) we covered two types of RFID handheld readers. Each is designed to read data stored on an UHF RFID tag from about 3 feet away when pointed at a tagged asset. We prefer the model featured in Figure (6.6) as it can read both barcode and RFID tags. However, there are tablets that clip onto a Sled that can also read barcodes. Chain of custody concerns with tablets is an issue.

12.5.4 Fixed Wall Mount RFID Antennas & Readers

RFID systems typically use antennas and multi-port readers as well as other devices covered in section (13.2.1). The ability of an RFID antenna to receive tag signals from a distance is dependent on their gain measured in dbiC. The "C" stands for Circularly Polarized Dipole Antenna. This type of antenna can read UHF tags from a wider range of lateral angles. The gain of an RFID reader is measured in dbm. This is important for reliability at ingress and egress portals as well as with RTLS applications. The term S.O.A.P. is commonly used in RFID applications. It stands for Size, Orientation, Angle, and Placement. Signal strength at various vantage points near portals on each floor within a facility is critical and for RTLS applications as well. Refer to section (13.2.2). Metal shelving and other obstacles can block RFID signals.

12.5.5   Date & Time Stamped Event Records – including integrated Video/RFID files

Without a date and time stamp on both video surveillance and RFID monitoring software snap shots those snap shots would be worthless for both evaluating operations or as evidence in the case of theft of company assets. You would be hard pressed to find software for such systems that does not include this feature.

We recommend you establish a policy for video file retention as well, similar to other files. Use of cloud based storage will allow you to extend time based files that might come in handy when needed years later.

12.5.6   Telematics

This term is employed to describe software for Fleet Management. High end systems track the whereabouts of fleet vehicles via GPS but also information about mileage, periods of use and by whom, safety records, gas consumption, preventive maintenance and repair as well as unit availability.

12.6   Incorporating Fire Code & Employee Safety

In previous chapters we covered NOX systems and mentioned how it integrated RFID with Video Surveillance. In recent years great advances have been made in NOX systems to incorporate security, personnel movement, power consumption, lighting, HVAC systems, fire and gas alarms, as well as policing doors and key portals. These systems make it possible to monitor all functions at one work station.

When installing security systems and related protocols it is necessary you do so while at the same time respecting local fire codes and personnel safety at all time. For example, you can have exits with alarms when use is unauthorized, but those doors still need to allow personnel to exit without restriction.

12.7   Defense Against Electronic Intrusion

In addition to all the compliance standards mentioned above in section 12.0 and their various sub-parts, where specific defenses are not covered, we've identified specific steps you can take to be pro-active as you draft your formal security plan.

Also, keep in mind no matter what you do if someone with the proper skill sets wants to get into your system it will happen. Reason being, there is only one of you and thousands of them – some are private individuals or groups some just intent on doing damage "for fun" and some for profit like those engaged in ransom demands as well as those that are sponsored by foreign governments. So the question is what can you do?

Of course step one is to install anti-virus software and step two is to establish a routine backup protocol and follow it. In addition to NAS/RAID backup systems you should backup to an external hard drive – one normally disconnected from your network system. Backup to the cloud is advisable as well. Remember any storage disk connected to a LAN network is exposed to hacking, including RAID drives.

Establish a protocol to do this, but immediately after you run a scan with your anti-virus software, before doing a dump to backup drives. Then, secure those drive(s). Beyond those steps, you will need to get into the specifics – some covered in the sub-parts below:

12.7.1   Anti-Virus Systems

In July of 2015 we were hit with a ransomware virus called, "TorrentLocker". According to Comcast* it was launched by a cybercrime gang operating out of Eastern Europe. It locked us out of nearly all of our files, except oddly enough the one application that we used to manage and record operations, FormFlow*. I suspect the reason for that is that it was an old program that ran on either 8-bit or 16-bit platform.

Payment to this gang was via Bitcoin. Fortunately, we had backed up most of the important files in a number of locations so although it took two weeks to put everything back in place, we recovered. We also used the opportunity to upgrade our OS, PCs, and server. So, no payment was made.

We had a leading anti-virus/internet security program installed in all our hardware, but it blew right through that software like it wasn't even there. At the time Comcast* was recommending to their customers to switch to MalwareBytes, so that's what we did and to date we have had zero problems. MWB has products for private use as well as for enterprises. They also offer VPN (Virtual Private Networks) services.

Paying close attention to your anti-virus/internet security systems in place is critical and getting even more critical as hacking continues to grow throughout the world. Larger companies, especially those engaged in sensitive projects should work very closely with companies like MWB and others to stay on top of threats.

12.7.2   Adopting Policies & Personnel Training

You can have the most advanced systems available on the market, but without policies for personnel you can still leave your company exposed to outside threats. More important, policies alone do little good unless your employees are trained to adhere to them. In addition, those policies and related directives as well as the training programs need to be well documented. Poor practices related to emails are an example how viruses can bypass security features. This includes opening emails, attachments, and clicking on links.

12.7.3   Backup & Redundancy

Drafting a system plan as well as operating protocols for back up and redundancy cannot be stressed enough. In addition to RAID software and hardware we recommend you consider both in-house backup as well as cloud storag e. Refer to chapter (4) and Network System Architecture Diagram displayed in Figure (4.2).

External storage drives that can be disconnected from all parts of your network can ensure those files will not get infected when malicious software penetrates your system. We even use WD My Passport* drives to backup big projects when in progress and completed, then keep those under lock and key as a third measure of redundancy.

12.7.4   UPS – Uninterruptable Power Supply

A UPS should be large enough to handle the load for your entire system grid. If you don't have a specifically laid out electrical grid for your computer, security, or other critical systems, then you should make sure you are protected from *Brown-Out* spikes. Spikes like the type displayed below, depending on the energy measured in Joules/sec, can fry those cheap Varistors used in most PC power supplies.

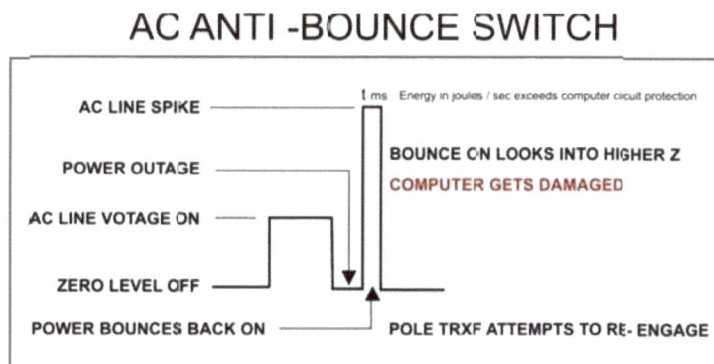

Figure 12.2

In other words, it is not so much the power going down that does the damage; instead, it's those momentary spikes when the utility transformers outside the facility tries to turn back ON – sometimes more than once. Those upward spikes can wipe out not only data, but PC workstation and server power supplies as well. A UPS needs to bring power back up quickly, but smoothly and protect against brown-outs.

12.7.5   Use of Passwords vs. Biometrics
Lately much has been made about how passwords are becoming unmanageable. Many users either keep them in Notepad files, easily accessed or worse yet in their pencil draw or taped to desk pullouts. Of course, this defeats the purpose entirely. Some people keep them in their wallet, but if it gets stolen, then you have a real problem. In recent years Biometrics has become very reliable and we recommend the use of biometrics as opposed to passwords whenever possible.

Some locked cabinets employ a combination of fingerprint biometrics and a four digit pin number. One such enclosure might be one used to store expensive RFID readers in your receiving or inventory area.

12.7.6   Log OFF After Use
It takes little effort or time to log OFF when workstations are not in use. Log-in screens also allow employees during one shift to prepare controlled entry for the next shift worker. This is an added measure of safety with respect to unauthorized entry, especially if each shift worker is required to enter via a password, pin number, or biometric. To ensure log off automatically go to Personalized setting using the Control Panel in your operating system.

12.7.7   Controlled Access to Specific Files & Data Fields
The EDMS (Electronic Document Management System) featured in this book and in examples in the Appendix has provision to control access to specific files as well as the ability to make edit to those files. Code or script can also be included to limit access and/or editing privileges to various data fields in each record. Most electronic records software or ERP systems offer the same capabilities.

12.7.8   Limit Characters in Text Based Data Fields
From the early days of computers and use of eForms I can remember one of the basic security practices that were stressed was to limit the number of characters that could be entered into text based data fields - the concept being, to prevent anyone from entering malicious code via the eForm itself.

12.7.9   Bluetooth – Beware of Dongles & External Repeaters
For security reasons we recommend not to use Bluetooth devices and to turn OFF Bluetooth capabilities on all workstations. AND if you find them necessary make sure you remove any Bluetooth Dongle when you're finished using it. Powerful external Repeaters attached to the outside of your building can be used to capture data and gain unauthorized entry through nearby workstations into your company's server with these devices left connected.

12.7.10   Faraday Shields
Some companies that include highly sensitive areas within their facilities, such as R&D lab or other control rooms employ Faraday Shields to block electromagnetic signals or EMI from external sources. This can be wire mesh or even EMI paint on walls and ceilings.

12.7.11   Use of VPN – Virtual Private Network
A VPN, or Virtual Private Network, allows you to create a secure connection to another network over the Internet. VPNs can be used to access region-restricted websites, corporate communications with franchised outlets or satellite location, or shield your browsing activity from prying eyes on public Wi-Fi, and more. Most operating systems have integrated VPN support.

12.7.12 Software - Back Doors
Back Doors when referring to software programs are typically defined as unpublished access ports to programs usually designed by the employee or contractor who originally wrote the program. They can have legitimate purposes, but when they are disclosed to others or in the hands of employees no longer working for your company they can result in major problems, especially without an NDA in place.

12.7.13 RFID Antennas
Any devices used to receive a coded signal and connected to your company LAN is weak spot. There is software that can allow data only formatted for its intended purpose. It is also possible to jam an RFID antenna and you can also install devices that can alarm your security when this occurs. More advanced systems have the ability to lock doors to those affects ports momentarily while security guards can investigate. Refer to section (13.3) for more information.

12.7.14 RFID Tag Security
The term "WORM" is defined (Write Once Read Many). Of course with this type of tag once written no changes can be made to its stored data. Although, the earlier tag versions included password protection, they were not totally full proof. The new EPC Class Gen 2 Version 2 tags include advanced password protection. Refer to section (5.5.4)

12.7.15 Entry via Power Supplies
With special equipment it's possible to hack into computer systems via your AC power line, at least to capture data. To prevent this companies that need protection from this type of evasion use *pi* filters. The industry refers to these filters as "Tempest Line Filters". Fact is, most PC power supplies are very cheaply made and can leak data, leaving companies wide open to data thief. Power lines in high security facilities engaged in sensitive work may be required to use NSA approved Tempest filters. However, the NSA classifies most TEMPEST standards.

TEMPEST is an acronym for (Telecommunications Electronics Material Protected from Emanating Spurious Transmissions). A tempest filter eliminates conducted EMI (Electro Magnetic Interference) information. Simply put, data is constantly being leaked through power lines and almost any other outlet that transmits electronic information. These filters are designed to stop it. Noise (data) can be conducted or radiated. TEMPEST filters cannot protect against radiated transmissions. The best way to stop radiated transmissions is with shielding, a faraday cage, or smart glass with signal blocking laminates - Smartgrad*.

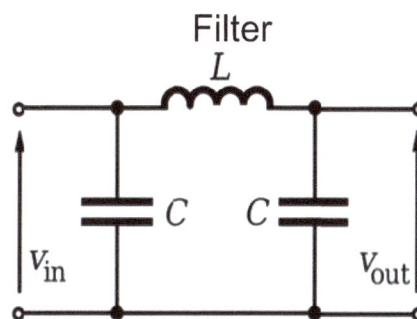

Figure 12.3

Note: Tempest filters are considerably more sophisticated than the simple *pi* filter displayed here, but the concept is the same.

Chapter 13 – RFID/Video Surveillance/Analytics - Integration

13.0 Overview

When laying out plans for systems related to RFID, Video Surveillance, and real time dashboard analytics, like Microsoft Power BI you need to realize the integration of such systems are not just for asset management, but also for security, safety, materials handling, and production management as well.

Systems like this will require a host of peripheral devices such as RFID antennas, RFID readers, audio communication, video cameras, sensors, motion detectors, door switches, alarms as well as POE network switches and computers to monitor it all. When you want to use other devices such as motion detectors or alarms with your RFID reader, you can use vacant ports on your GPIO adaptor to report back to security monitors via that RFID reader via a network switch. To wire the system over long distances throughout your facility you will also need hubs and POE extenders. GPIO modules come with 4, 8, or even 64 port channels. An iPIO device is a cloud based device.

Technology is being introduced almost faster than you can keep up with it, but remember applicability requires careful review before you jump in with both feet. Practicality for your business is also an issue to consider, especially when it comes to cost and maintenance – both in the way of installation and support resources, including personnel. In other words, Cost-Benefit Analysis still applies.

If you plan to embrace dashboard analytics, remember this information does not flow back to a control monitor without sensors and/or photocells located at each feeder or primary assembly line or point where information is being collected. If you want to also view real time activity from either a desktop monitor or mobile device from those points, IP or WIFI video cameras will be required there as well. So, it's not just the analytics software, it's a major commitment in infrastructure and its maintenance.

That said, we recommend even the smallest company impediment and maintain a basic system for proper asset management. This includes at a minimum serialized and barcoded property labels, receiving logs, property records, and asset disposition reports for lost or life ended assets as well as regular inventory audits. With respect to security we also recommend, at minimum security cameras at each ingress and egress port and alarms at each exit only door throughout your facility. How you store that date/time stamped video data is optional, whether it's DVR, NVR, computer Hard Drive or a cloud based solution.

As mentioned, remember UHF RFID tags are relatively cheap, so even though you don't plan on installing RFID antennas and readers anytime soon, if they are placed on assets items at the outset it will be much easier to install an RFID system later. Your assets will already be tagged written to with a tag EPC and ID. Refer to Chapter (5), section (5.6).

13.1 RFID System

There are basically three ways to use RFID: (1) is to use RFID on boxes or products to control movement on a conveyer belt for material handling purposes; (2), to use RFID at portals (ingress and egress points) within your facility to monitor movement of tag assets or inventory; and (3) to use RFID RTLS (Real Time Locating Systems) to track movement of assets and/or product within your plant or facility.

The ladder use (RTLS) employs multiple RFID antennas mounted on walls in each room or staging area to track movement via a method called, "Trilateration" where the subject tag is pinged to fix its location.

13.1.1 RFID Antennas
There are basically two types of RFID antennas - Linear and Circular Polarized. The term Linear means the antenna emits and receives RF signals in a straight line. A Circular Polarized antenna emits and receives an RF signal using a cone shaped pattern that widens away from the antenna. There are two basic types of Circular Polarized antennas: RHCP (Right Hand Circular Polarized) and LHCP (Left Hand Circular Polarized).

If two antennas are facing each other one should be a RHCP (Right Hand Circular Polarized) antenna and the other a LHCP (Left Hand Circular Polarized) antenna. This prevents null spots in the read field when a multipath condition occurs when a direct RF wave intersects with another RF wave with a different phase. Using Bistatic antennas at each read zone or portal will reduce this type of EMI.

The definition of *multipath* is when two or more favorable radio paths exist between the reader antenna and the tag. This could be caused by a reflection off of a metal object in the or near the read zone. When the reader sends a signal to the antenna to 'ping the tag' the antenna doesn't just send one beam of RF waves straight forward. The reader antenna sends waves on several different paths in order to pick up the tag's signal. This is where reflection, refraction, diffraction, and absorption come into play.

Figure 13.1 *Courtesy of Impinj*

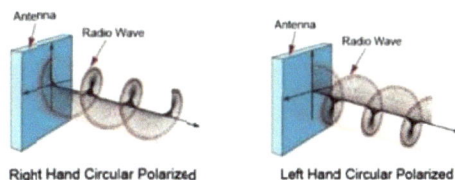

Figure 13.2 *Courtesy of Atlas RFID*

13.1.2 RFID Readers
There are basically two types of RFID readers, "Monostatic" and "Bistatic". A Monostatic reader has only one type of antenna port – for both transmitting (pinging) and receiving an RF signal. A Bistatic reader has a pair of antenna ports – one for pinging and one for receiving a signal from the pinged tag.

Figure 13.3 *Courtesy of Impinj*

13.1.3 RFID Hubs
An RFID hub expands the number of antennas you can connect to one RFID reader. For example, using a hub with 8 antennas ports will allow you to connect 32 antennas off of one 4 port RFID reader. A diagram of this example is displayed in section (13.1.9) in Figure 13.X.

Figure 13.4   *Courtesy of Impinj*

13.1.4 RFID GPIO Adaptors
The term GPIO is an acronym that stands for (General Purpose Input Output). GPIO adaptors and modules working together with antenna hubs allow you to multiplex a larger number of antennas off each reader port as well as allow sensors like motion detector to work in tandem with RFID antennas. For example, RFID software programs like Clearstream* can be programmed by the user to link a specific motion detector to a specific portal antenna y device ID number. Other sensors can be used in a similar manner, like alarms, weight sensors, multi-colored stack lights, or other sensors as well. Clearstream* (Version 4) can also limit the RFID receiver ON time in seconds to limit the signals received without surrounding interference signals or by only etting the strongest signal through. This also reduces the data storage time when recording this sentry information. Refer to multiplexed antenna schema in section (13.1.9). As an example, you could omit the last antenna an use some of the inputs from the GPIO for one or two motion sensors. GPIOs also give you bidirectional control as well; for example, turning ON a color coded stack light. GPIO boxes or PCB modules have up to 64 channels, each with their own port ID.

Figure 13.5   *Courtesy of Impinj*

13.1.5 iPIO
This acronym stands for (Internet Protocol Input Output) device. It's used to transmit event information through the cloud from more than one or multiple locations.

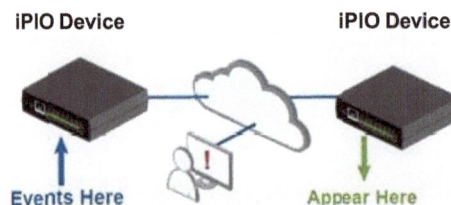

Figure 13.6   *Courtesy of KVM Switches*

The **iPIO** is a **network** attached, web   enabled digital input and output device. The **iPIO** can be and monitored with a standard web browser. Multiple **iPIO** devices can communicate amongst them selves to transport I/O information across the **network.**

13.1.6 POE Extenders

Some RFID readers based on their power output measured in dbm - used to define signal strength in wires and cables. Most readers can transmit signals up to about 300 feet to a network switch. Beyond that you will need a POE Extender before the POE cable reaches a network switch.

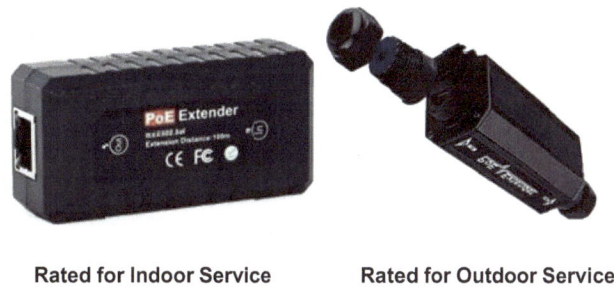

Rated for Indoor Service   Rated for Outdoor Service

Figure 13.7

13.1.7 Cable, Connectors, and Raceways

POE Cat 5e cable is the most popular for most RFID wiring applications. POE Cat 5e is now available with a Foil shielding – in both indoor and outdoor rated jackets.

When cutting Cat 5e pull out cable for systems wiring a pass through RJ45 connector is used. Before you cut the excess wired off at the front of the connector you can arrange them to fix whatever protocol schema you using.

To protect cables from damage and/or unauthorized access, raceways are typically employed.   These are available in a variety of materials for both interior and exterior use.

Ethernet Cable

	Category 3	Category 5	Category 5e	Category 6	Category 6a	Category 7
Cable Type	UTP	UTP	UTP	UTP or STP	STP	S/FTP
Max. Data Transmission Speed	10 Mbps	10/100/1000 Mbps	10/100/1000 Mbps	10/100/1000 Mbps	10000 Mbps	10,000 Mbps
Max. Bandwidth	16 MHz	100 MHz	100 MHz	250 MHz	500 MHz	600 MHz

Cat 5e – Available in FTP (Foil Shielded)

RJ45 Pass Through Ethernet Connector

Typical Interior Raceway

Figure 13.8

13.1.8 Signal Strength Meters

When testing RFID reading zones using UHF tags and various antennas a signal strength meter is often used to ensure tagged items or tagged employee ID badges get read properly. For example, objects like metal shelving or other obstacles may need to be removed from reading zones to prevent reflection to maximize signal strength and/or prevent reflection, refraction diffraction and absorption.

Figure 13.9 *Courtesy of Vulcan RFID*

13.1.9 RFID System Diagrams

The wiring scheme displayed in this diagram will allow you to multiplex 32 RFID Antennas with one 4-port RFID reader. Obviously, if you employ a Bistatic RFID Reader with separate pinging and receiving ports this scheme would have to change and alternate hubs would be devoted to either antennas used for pinging or receiving signals at each portal.

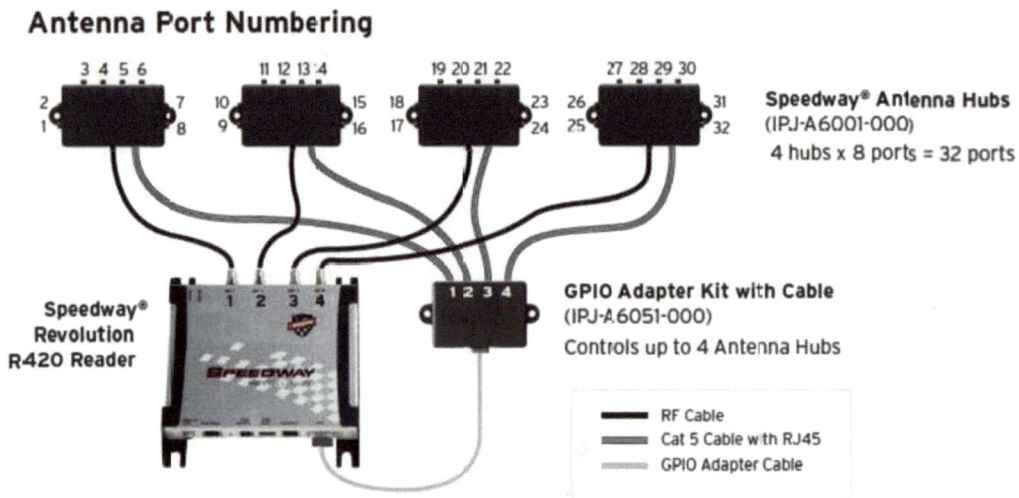

Figure 13.10 *Courtesy of Impinj*

The type of cable used and where is detailed in this diagram. You can run POE (Power-Over-Ethernet) Cat5e cable up to about 300 feet. Beyond that you will need a signal extender or booster, before the cable reaches you Network Switch and/or security monitors. Refer to section (13.1.6). Impinj* Speedway Connect Software is designed to work with the Speedway RFID Reader and other hardware displayed above.

One of the leading suppliers of RFID devices is the Atlas RFID Store https://www.atlasrfidstore.com/. They also have a wealth of information on their site to assist you with installation of RFID systems.

13.1.10 Software - NOX

A smaller businesses might employ software like Clearstream* mentioned in section (13.1.4) to set up and monitor a facility wide RFID system. As mentioned this software features the ability to combine the use of motion detectors, alarms, or other sensors. For example, if an RFID antenna picked up an asset near an fire exit door a motion sensor would alert security and the alarm would sound near that fire exit to alert personnel someone was using an unauthorized exit. That security based software is part of any Asset Management System designed to protect and track property moving in and out of a facility.

Usually smaller businesses will install at a minimum, a video surveillance system. It could be a *Closed Circuit TV* system with CCTV cameras and a DVR to record footage, or use IP or WIFI cameras and a NVR or cloud service to store recording for access remotely. Obviously, the ladder is more desirable and facilitates the use of mobile devices.

A simple NOX system combines RFID and Video Surveillance in one software program where a picture of anyone entering without a RFID tagged employee ID badge or exiting with an asset on their person. It then date and time stamps the event for use by security and/or HR should disciplinary action be required.

NOX is one element is what is referred to as a Software Defined Networking (SDN) ecosystem. It's basically an open source platform for building network control applications using C++ programming. It can combine many control functions like security based RFID, Video Surveillance, and controls for HAVC, Fire, Temperature, lighting, energy consumption as well as other facility monitoring and control services. This is where facilities management is going, especially for larger companies. So when software firms use the term NOX today they are most likely referring to a fully integrated monitoring and control system.

13.2 Foiling RFID Systems

As a responsible author I debated whether or not to include this information, but after searching the web it was clear this information is readily available for all to see – including bad actors. There are a number of ways to foil an RFID system, but I'll cover the two that are most common:

One is to use a signal jammer. However, devices are available today to detect and alert security when a jammer signal is being picked up by an RFID antenna AND with Video Surveillance you can see who is lurking near that antenna and security can take action.

The second method and probably the most common used by employees up to no good or anyone trying to exit with tagged company assets is to use a metal or EMI screen, like a copper lined bag or briefcase. Actually, such bags and briefcases are sold for preventing near the person carrying the bag or briefcase from reading data on personal devices. The problem is products like this have a dual purpose.

You should also know that cyber criminals have been known to hack RFID tags to plant viruses on computer networks so when you write to tags make sure you include passwords or better yet a WORM tag. As mentioned in Chapter 5, EPC Class Gen 2 Version 2 tags feature improved password protection. Refer to https://www.gs1.org for current information.

13.3 Video Surveillance System

This section will cover the various types of video cameras as well as their advantages and disadvantages. Most businesses will opt for IP Video cameras which are for the most part maintenance free. When emergency generators kick in it's advisable to have them provide power immediately to computer system and all RFID, Video Surveillance, fire control, and other critical facility ecosystems.

13.3.1 CCTV, IP, and WIFI Cameras

There are three types of video surveillance cameras available: (1) CCTV; (2), IP; and (3), WIFI. A description of each is provided here:

- CCTV (Close Circuit TV) is an analog camera and is wired using coaxial cable and BNC connectors and its recording is stored in a DVR.

- IP Video Cameras are digital and are typically wired with Ethernet cable like POE Cat 5e which carries the power and data back to a network switch and a NVR (Network Video Recorder) or to a cloud storage service. Those recordings are also available on demand by authorized personnel from either a remote work station or mobile device when motion detectors set off alarms. These cameras are also hard wired and therefore low maintenance.

- WIFI Video Cameras are digital and operate off their own battery power which means those batteries will need to be replaced or charged at regular intervals. To conserve power they are typically motion activated and their signal is received by a nearby router, if close enough to pick up that signal. If not, then a number of RF repeaters will be required throughout the facility.

Although, GPIO modules can be used for motion detectors, switches, or alarms reporting wherever RFID antennas are receiving RFID signals, or where video surveillance cameras are located, when using IP with built-in motion sensors it may not be required, especially when those cameras are reporting back directly to a network switch to the security monitor(s). WIFI video cameras are susceptible to signal jammers.

13.3.2 Splitters

Splitters are used to split video signals or data so two IP video surveillance cameras can operate off one network cable going back to a network switch.

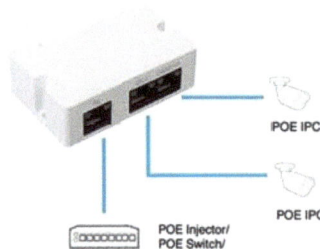

Figure 13.11 *Courtesy of Linovision*

13.3.3 Camera Locations & Positions

One of the main reasons for a splitter at a video surveillance site or facility portal is to locate two cameras so that one captures the face of the person either coming or going through that portal or exit. Without a view of the person's face even with a date/time stamped RFID tag data identifying the asset item it may be impossible to prosecute a bad actor.

13.3.4 Video Surveillance Software

There are a number of sources for video surveillance software. Xeoma* is a brand sold by Amazon and is sold at various price points depending on the number of cameras it can handle. This software program will work with CCTV, IP, and WIFI video cameras. Other brands are: Blue Iris, Ivideon Server, SmartViewer, ZoneMinder, Freedom VMS, Contaware ContaCam, SGS HomeGuard, and Visec Surveillance Software.

13.4 MS Power BI/Video Integrated Systems

As production lines and other manufacturing processes become more mechanized and automated dashboard analytics are becoming an integral part of operations management, not only reporting methods on final assembly lines, but also n all feeder lines and operations supporting final assembly.

Microsoft P ower BI is one such software program that can not only provide operation managers with dashboard data for all points on the production floor, but also provide a real time view of those operations using video surveillance cameras at all key points through the factory floor.   This allows managers to monitor output and spot bottlenecks in flow.   Here is a screen shot of a MS Power BI dashboard with video surveillance, monitoring real time activity on the floor of an auto production line:

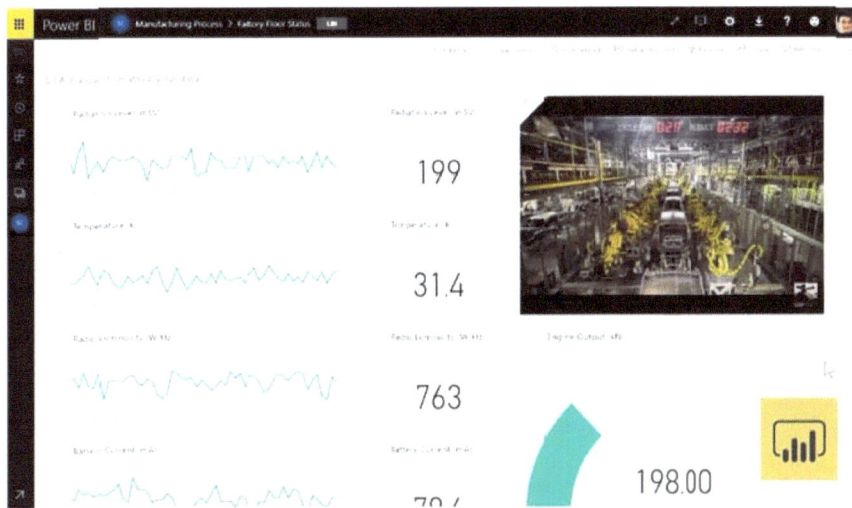

Figure 13.12   *Courtesy of Microsoft Power BI*

13.5 IT Operations – a total spectrum approach

IT operations are growing in scope every year, both with respect to network architecture as well as operations. It would be very difficult for a business to embrace security systems like RFID, Video Surveillance, and facility related ecosystems without realizing how they all relate to IT in addition to IT's traditional role.

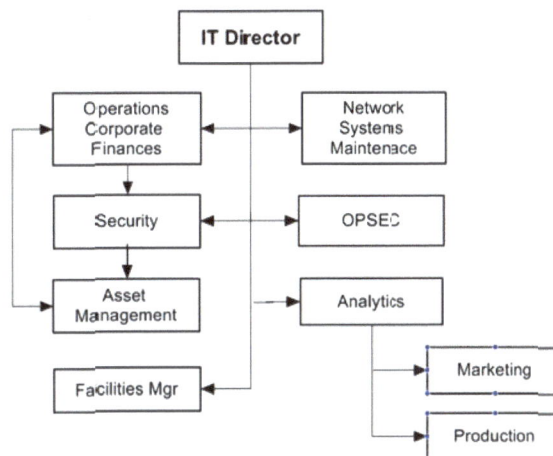

Figure 13.13

13.5.1 IT

Information technology (IT) is the use of any computers, software, storage, networking, and other physical devices, infrastructure and processes to create, process, store, retrieve, secure, and exchange all forms of electronic data. IT operations typically support executive management, corporate finance, and all departments within a business enterprise as well as manage activities with its distributors and customers.

13.5.2 OPSEC

The term is defined as Operations Security - a process for protecting critical information. This used to be a military term, but private industry today is faced with so many internal and external threats it has become a science for government and private industry as well as an integral part of IT operations. It involves the following steps:

- Identify critical information
- Analyze Threats
- Analyze Vulnerabilities
- Assess Risks with each
- Apply appropriate countermeasures

13.5.3 Facility Management - ecosystems

Facility Management is no longer just about helping to design or layout production staging areas, preventative maintenance of a building's utilities or equipment, but now as covered in section (13.1.10) with NOX and other automated software and hardware systems it covers a facilities entire ecosystem. As such events and data related the facility's ecosystem is very much a part of IT operations.

13.5.4 Security

Security may take many forms depending on the nature and size of a business enterprise. Hopefully, at the very least it will include video surveillance. To protect its assets and control movement in and out of its facility it may also include an RFID system as well as motion detectors and alarms at each fire exit. Security for many businesses will also include monitoring and control of its facilities ecosystem.

13.5.5 AMS – Asset Management Systems

The term Asset Management System is obviously tied to a business's accounting system with respect to cost recovery or depreciation, including amortization of intangibles like software or various agreements. However, security and facilities management are also part of any Asset Management System, as is IT operations and record keeping practices.

13.5.6 Analytics

The term Analytics today has become a science not only as it relates to marketing, but production as well as other aspects of a business enterprise. Whether a business is tracking the cost benefit related to advertising to manage its ongoing Customer Acquisition Cost or spotting bottlenecks in production as feeder lines are driving primary or final assembly lines IT must be involved whenever this data is being collected and analyzed. To capture source data while processes are being completed photo-cells, other sensors of all kinds, event counters, recorders (human or machine), and even programmable logic controllers may be used.

All of these individual elements above must be overseen by IT in order to ensure they are adequately designed and maintained to meet the needs of the business enterprise and its various departments. AND of course, since each one of these elements are potentially a back door into a business enterprise's network server, risk assessment (OPSEC) can only be properly coordinated from the top down.

Chapter 14 – Dealing with Bad Actors

14.0 Overview

The best defense against employee thief, damage, or loss is a carefully drafted employment agreement, GAAP based records, and routine periodic audits as well as security systems like RFID/Video Surveillance and GPS/Telematics. We also recommend an employee handbook, making your company policies known..

Accountability can mean three actions in order of severity: (1) prosecute an employee; (2), fire an employee; and (3), recover loss by way of docking an employee's wages or severance pay. See Risk Assessment below.

Dealing with a bad actor requires policies, directives, and a documented process to avoid blow back in the way of law suits or other negative repercussions. Any confrontations with employees regarding missing or stolen assets should always be done in a private room and with your HR Director, the department head and/or supervisor present. Managers should be instructed to refrain from disclosing anything to other employees or outsiders. This is recommended whether the meeting is only an inquiry or the Exit Interview.

Action taken can range from "making a mountain out of a mole hill" to "…she took how much?!!!" Typically, the damage should dictate the course of action you take. If you have shareholders you must weigh your fiduciary responsibility against the economic cost of pursuing various courses of action. If your course of action makes economic sense then fine, but if it does not, your shareholders would not want you to throw good money after bad or expose the company to potential legal action. Then, there is a host of risk assessment issues to consider and that's where solid evidence is required.

You'll find it is a lot easier to gather evidence against an embezzler than an employee engaged in petty theft of physical assets. Money, other than petty cash, always leaves a money trail if you know how to find it. In today's world of ecommerce and next day deliveries there should be no need for petty cash drawers in business. My advice is to get rid of them entirely.

When dealing with theft of physical assets, eye witness accounts may not be enough. Eye witness accounts can be written off in court as workplace tension between employees, where video surveillance tapes are final. If the assets taken are small enough to hide under a coat, then a combo RFID/Video Surveillance system will be required at each exit within your facility to record and time stamp the incident. Other than this level of surveillance, GAAP based internal controls can be used to identify missing assets depending on the frequency of audits, but even with strict chain of custody records it's difficult to accuse anyone in particular, unless you transfer employees who may be suspected and remove their access for a period of time.

Although, your first thought may be to call the police and prosecute the thief, you may want to first contemplate your course of action. Instead of blaming the employee, you would be wise to instead blame yourself for not having proper controls in place to prevent the theft or not doing a good enough job in screening the subject employee. This may be the only way you will learn to improve your defenses. After that you should make an informed decision regarding you course of action. That is what this chapter is all about. For example, would it be wise to spend money on attorneys or on added surveillance going forward?

14.1 Vetting Candidates for Employment

Pre-employment drug testing was unheard of prior to the 1980s, but with mores declining in our modern day society it has become standard practice, along with a growing list of other pre-employment screening.

For example, in addition to any history of embezzlement or thief, an employer needs to be aware of job candidates who have a history of working just long enough to file a claim of a workplace injury to abuse the LNI (Labor and Industries) or worker's Compensation Insurance, causing your LNI tax rate to skyrocket. These folks will often move from state to state. Fortunately, for employers today there are private screening agencies that can provide you with this history as well as other character traits. See section 14.1.4 below.

Although, most employers would like to believe those that apply for work with their company are just honest folks looking to make a living for them and their family, the sad fact according to Chron is that 75% of all employees will steal at least once from their employer and 37% of those will steal repeatedly until caught. So pre-employment screening has become a requirement; concept being, if the list of character traits listed in section 14.1.4 comes back positive that person is an honest, trustworthy, and forthright individual. If not, you may expect problems and your risk level for loss increases.

14.1.1 Interviewing Process

Most employers would agree, their company is only as good as their employees. In terms of assets, they are the most valuable asset in any company. Therefore, before inviting anyone onto the team it requires a careful, deliberate, and documented recruiting and selection process. It has become standard practice for employers to interview candidates for employment at least two, three, or more times prior to hiring them. The number of interviews may vary based on the size of the company or organization.

Of course the interview process starts with drafting an updated job description and a recruiting ad with minimum qualifications or certifications for the position, approved by management and all those in the process: CEO/COO, HR Director, Department Head, and the supervisors. Today you have the option of posting that recruiting ad with a local newspaper, professional/trade journals, or with one or more search engines with job listings like INDEED*, GLASSDOOR*, ZIPRECRUITER* or others. Each will vary in cost and efficacy. We recommend you record your success with each for subsequent use.

As you gather resumes a preliminary weeding process will be required. If your HR Director is given the task it will require management draft criteria for that process. For example, you may wish to omit all those whose resumes display a history of short tenure with the previous employers listed. You should also list who on the team should participate in the preliminary interview, and each interview thereafter during the entire selection process as well as who votes to make the final decision.

To protect the company from employee disputes we recommend adding a disclaimer to all job descriptions stating, *"The duties and responsibilities described are not a comprehensive list and that additional tasks may be assigned to the employee from time to time and/or the scope of the job may change as necessitated by business demands"*. We recommend you consult with your corporate attorney prior to using this disclaimer.

Of course, a disclaimer will do you no good if the employee claims he or she was never provided with a copy of it or other documents such as an employment agreement or the employee handbook. Therefore, a list of all such handouts should be confirmed on a listing form with the employee's signature for future reference. A copy should be attached to the employee's file and included in the packet of materials given to all new hires.

14.1.2 Adopting a Path Based on Cost

Obviously, background checks are not cheap; therefore, if there is any testing involved in the selection process and the company can conduct that testing itself, you'll want to start with that first before you spend money on background checks.

14.1.3 Testing & Pre-employment Qualifications

Question: Is it legal to require that applicants pass a written test? Answer is yes, but only if the same test is given to all employees applying for the same job - a good reason not to let copies of it or the correct answers get out. We recommend a multiple choice test to eliminate any ambiguity.

Coming from the medical device market after informing applicants a written test would be required, I recall how some applicants ask if that was illegal while some actually bolted. Fact is, it is not only legal, but a requirement of the FDA (QSR 820.25) as well as necessary to remain in compliance with either ISO 9001 (subpart 7.2) or ISO 13485(subpart 6.2) Quality Management System (QMS) standards.

We administered the same test to both our electronic technicians as we did for our electrical engineers. This test included basic questions related to DC and AC Ohms Law. We always provided each applicant with both a pocket calculator and a cheat sheet with the necessary Ohms Law formulas. It was our experience those with college degrees failed where those techs returning from the U.S. Navy aced this test.

After 50 years in business you tend to experience a lot of things the general public is never made aware of. I recall an incident where we interviewed five real clean cut college graduates – nice kids. I was shocked when they failed this simple DC/AC Ohms Law test. All these kids where from a well known university in the area and had just graduated with a degree in electrical engineering. I immediately called other members of our trade association (American Electronics Association) in the area to ask if this is what they were experiencing. They reported to me this was common knowledge among other local employers in the industry and they were putting these kids on tech benches to start and sending them through their own retraining programs. It would be another two years before they would let them onto a product development teams. Our needs were more immediate. We finally hired a young man from a smaller college who aced the test. So, make of that what you will, but testing is well worth it.

14.1.4 Background Checks

When you narrow your selection process down to the applicant you think is the best fit for your company and the position available, you can then contract with an agency to perform a background check. The checks listed below are typical. Needless to say this information should be kept under lock and key and never disclosed to anyone, including the applicant except to HR and top management.

- Certifications, confirming all educational achievements and/or certifications listed on the resume
- Drug Use or Substance Abuse
- Criminal Record
- Court Records, including domestic abuse
- Sexual Offenses
- LNI History
- Credit Rating, including law suits, liens, bankruptcies, and evictions
- Driving Record, including accidents or DUIs

Whether or not an applicant is bondable will depend on his or her position with your company and can only be determined by the agency providing the Fidelity Bond. If you plan on securing a Fidelity Bond on an applicant, normally that bonding agency will do their own background check. However, you may want to inquire if the list above is included. If not, you may want to contract with a separate agency (i.e. driving record, LNI history, etc.) Some recognized agencies are listed in the reference section of this chapter.

14.2   Gathering Proof

Before you can gather proof of either embezzlement or theft of physical assets you must proper GAAP based internal controls and related record to first detect and then deduce who may be responsible. If it's embezzlement you can follow the money trail. However, unless you catch someone trying to remove an item from your facility the only good way is to have a video surveillance system in place or better yet, a combination RFID/Video surveillance system to record the item passing by the antenna along with a time stamped still photo of the employee leaving. Refer to sections (12) and (13).

Often GAAP based controls and related records offer what amounts to a Chain of Custody record to detect when and where in the process the item went missing or never made it to the next step in the process. Of course, if the asset made it through the entire process and was placed in service for some period, it may be more difficult to find it, unless other employees on the floor in the vicinity notice it's missing the immediately report it to their supervisor.

What some companies do is maintain a list of online consumer to consumer ecommerce sales sites like ebay, Craig's List, and look for listing of those items missing and have someone purchase the item and inspect it for a serial number. Another way is to visit local pawn shops for the items missing and pose as an interested customer.

Of course, without a Property Record with make, model, and serial number it will do you little good unless you can produce an invoice with the serial number. If the asset item missing is of little value, it may not even be worth the time spent.

In case the thief removed the *Property-of* label and the serial tag another way is to hide an RFID tag somewhere inside the asset and use an RFID reader to reveal the item belongs to your company or organization, and then call the police. If you don't have an RFID surveillance system or antennas at each exit in your facility, this is something that we recommend doing, especially with more expensive physical assets.

It's common place for computers and laptops to have GPS tracking devices in them and of course with fleet cars that has become standard operating procedure. It would also be wise to install GPS in large machinery or expensive equipment, so when it's plugged back in or turned ON you can track its new location for the authorities. The trick is to install it where it's hard to see it, but in a location where the signal is not shielded.

Furthermore, even if you are able to collect proof of theft by an employee or a group of employees, depending on the value and how you format and present that proof may determine whether the authorities will even bother to prosecute. In most large cities police detectives normally have a stack of case files they must work through and are often shorthanded. The backlog could go out for months. The first question the police may ask is if you have a fidelity bond or other insurance.

In order to get either police or DA to move on your case, depending on the value lost you may have to present the evidence in a format they can act on without a lot of leg work. If the case is large enough you may have to spend more money with your corporate attorney to help you with that task.

In the end you may have to turn to a civil suit and that will cost you money and that's assuming you win. Even with a judgement in hand it may be like "squeezing blood out of a turnip", as they say.

For example, some years ago one of our trademarks was coming up for renewal with the USPTO. I managed the files for a number of our product related trademarks so I was very familiar with the renewal notice and renewal form the USPTO sends out. I knew one was coming due soon, so when I got what appeared to be their official envelope with the return address: United State Patent and Trademark Office. I immediately had a check cut and sent them $375.00. I did notice the *Payable-To* address was located in Los Angeles, CA but I knew the USPTO had recently opened offices there so I assumed that was where they were processing renewal payments. I was a little confused when I kept getting renewal notices for the same trademark so I called the USPTO to find out they never received my payment. When I told the USPTO representative where I sent the money, she informed me that I was scammed. Apparently, anyone can order a list of trademark due for renewal and then use that list to race ahead of the USPTO to divert the payment to them. It was a PO Box but the USPTO also uses a PO Box.

So, finally realizing we had been scammed, I made a PDF copy of the envelope, the phony renewal form, the real renewal form used by the USPTO, which was identical, and a copy of both sides of our processed check. Then I called the FBI and talked to a secretary in their Seattle Office. I told her if you move fast before they changed their PO Box, one of your agents in Los Angeles should be able to catch them. I was shocked when she said, "Oh sir, we don't do that". So, I asked her if you don't go after folks ripping off inventors and trademark holders purporting to be the USPTO, just what do you guys do? I followed that call by filling out the online form the Postal Inspection Service has on their website, but I never heard back.

Then about seven months later I got a call from the USPTO and person on the other end of the call claimed to be a contract attorney working for the USPTO and asked me to send her PDF copies of the scam. She said a large number of inventors and trademark holders were ripped off, and even the USPTO was having trouble getting the FBI or any other enforcement authority to move on it, so the USPTO was preparing a presentation for a senate sub-committee. Again, I never heard back.

This is a true story. I have an entire file on the incident. So, it may give you some idea how badly our system is broken. So, as far as misappropriations or missing assets are concerned it is far better to be proactive and install the necessary security systems as opposed on relying on the authorities after the fact.

14.3 Employment Laws – Federal & State

Federal employment laws actually provide employers more rights when dealing with bad actors then some state laws. For example, federal laws may allow you to withhold severance pay or even deduct pay where some state laws may not allow it. Although, your attorney may advise you don't hold back any pay or do anything that would give a bad actor grounds for countersuit or put you in violation of state laws. A lot has to do with how well you write both your Employee Handbook and/or your Employment Agreement.

To avoid such problems an employer can always tell the subject employee he or she is being let go due to a slow or anticipated slowdown in business. Of course, remember where a dismissal due to a policy violation or criminal can prevent the state from increasing your SUTA experience rate or tax premium, a layoff may not.

To avoid penalty imposed by the state for layoffs many employers will establish a baseline in order to weather cyclical downturns in the economy and hire temps for all their needs above that baseline level. If you employ temps that may cause the employee or his union to question your actions, so you need to be ready for that.

Where you may be taking a big chance withholding pay or threatening to withhold pay until stolen items are returned or restitution is made for assets taken, for sure you would be more justified if severance pay was withheld until all items consigned to an employee in the normal course of business were returned, such as those items consigned by HR when an employee is first hired and signed a receipt for items; even more so, if the terms are spelled out in the Employee Handbook or an Employment Agreement.

Then there is the issue of intangible assets or unauthorized IP theft or transfer. That's where the terms in an Employee Handbook and/or Employment Agreement can save you. Without something in writing prohibiting theft of intangible property or defining what that property is can leave an employer without recourse. Once you put the employee's new employer on notice that the IP or Trade Secret is yours, you may have recourse with that third party. For that reason, most third party employers will stay clear of such disputes.

14.4   Courts & Legal Action

Non-compete clauses in Employment Agreements are harder to enforce, unless you can prove the employee used IP in his or her business after they leave your company or organization or sold or licensed it to others.

If you take legal action against either the employee or his or her new employer that may start by getting a judge to issue a temporary injunction or TRO (Temporary Restraining Order) preventing the sale, license, or use of the IP in question. That may buy you time, but if that action doesn't cause the bad actor or his new employer to capitulate you will have to go to court to seek remedy. The best advice we can give you is to seek legal counsel before taking any action. Each state has its own laws.

In some states like California, if the action is against a former employee, the TRO petition may be viewed to restrain legitimate competition and such action is prohibited by the state. You must prove your action is not just an attempt to restrain competition or trade, but is due to IP theft that will cause irreparable harm to your company or organization. The terms in your Employment Agreement and any investment in the IP you can quantify will weigh heavily.

14.5   Risk Assessment Practices – Preparing for Blowback

As an employer you may have already noticed when you call another employer for a reference that employer will only give you from-to dates worked and job title held and not much more information. The reason for this is that we live in a very litigious society. Also, employees have rights too – especially when they are innocent. However, this is also why the use of background checks has grown in popularity.

The first thing you want to do is to alert your IT Director or manager to immediately change access codes to computer files the subject employee may have. That will alert the employee something is wrong so if you're going to dismiss him or her you'll want to do it immediately thereafter. That is usually done with the HR Director, Department Head, and Supervisor in a private room where the Exit Interview is conducted. We recommend the employee be escorted off the premises and all those in the meeting be sworn to secrecy as it relates to other employees. You don't want to give a bad actor any grounds for defamation of character.

However, if you let the employee go for cause he or she will soon find out about it when the state unemployment benefits are withheld for (10) weeks or the appropriate waiting time. That period may vary with each state. That's usually when legal threats are made or actions occur.

We had to let a young woman go for embezzlement. Luckily we caught it early, after only $600 was taken when she was asked to fill in for a payroll clerk on vacation.

As soon as she realized she was not going to get her unemployment benefits or that they would be delayed she ran right out and hired a roadside attorney to threaten legal action in a written letter. We asked for a telephone conference with the state unemployment office and with them and her in the same room she was telling them how unfair we were being to her. At that point, I asked her if she had told people there about her embezzlement. She was not the sharpest knife in the drawer and said, "I was going to put it right back". Then I said, "is that why you recorded a different amount in the check register? You could hear the case officers in the background go whoa! The case officers, said "thank you sir I think we got all we need". That ended that case. We responded to her lawyer's letter and explained what happened and told him we would be happy to defend our actions and counter sue for damages. We never heard back. Apparently, she thought she could embezzle money from the company and the worst case if caught would be she'd get her unemployment benefits. She didn't realize there was a waiting-period for those who are let go for misconduct. It was too late to issue a stop order at our bank, so we wrote our losses off – not worth pursuing.

The most important thing you will require when letting an employee go for misconduct, theft, or misappropriation of funds is to gather proof and put it in a packet in timeline order – one a prosecuting attorney can use. This may include performance reports. Even with solid proof, often it will be an uphill battle and a costly one to get full restitution. This is where a first class security system can be helpful and maybe prevent the loss before it gets big enough to need a lawyer or the authorities. The other option is a fidelity bond for employees handling money. You may not always be covered by a fidelity bond, especially when bonded employees go on vacation and other employees fill in. In these cases you need to inspect their work product after each work assignment.

14.6   Fidelity Bonds – Audit Preparation
A Fidelity Bond is simply put, an insurance policy protecting you against employee thief or embezzlement of company funds. It's often referred to as a "commercial crime policy". The medium cost for a $1M policy is about $90 to $100 per month. A policy for $100K is about $25 per month. These policies vary so read the fine print and have it reviewed by your attorney.

As referenced in case law at the end of this chapter in a typical Fidelity Bond, coverage does not cover intangible property such as violation of licensing agreements, intellectual property, or industrial espionage.

14.6.1   Internal Controls
When establishing the premium for a Fidelity Bond the company providing the bond will want to review your GAAP based Internal Controls, the nature of your business, and the quality of the employee(s) you are bonding. They may want your company to include a "subrogation" clause in your Employment Agreement allowing then to subrogate legal action with the employee on the company's behalf. Obviously, an employee with a criminal record or embezzlement in the past will be reason for denial. The only exception to that rule is the Federal Bonding Program the Department of Labor has established for "at-risk" job seekers. The need for close supervision and limited access in cases like this as well as board approval are a given. There are a host of considerations when hiring "at-risk' employees, including potential liabilities with other employees.

14.6.2   Employee Records
Regardless of the Internal Controls your company has in place, including segregation of duties or a double set of eyes on each transaction, the insurance company will normally require a background check on each employee covered. See section 14.1.4 for the range of historical records investigated.

Again, it goes without saying, employee records whether they be background checks, performance, medical, or personal contact records should be protected under lock and key or password protected. This will normally include a NDA with your HR Director or anyone handling employee records within your company.

References:

Agencies that perform background checks:
Hire Right   https://www.hireright.com/
SentryLink   https://www.sentrylink.com

A number of online people search directories also offer limited background checks.

Insurance firms that provide Fidelity Bonds:
Pro-Surety Bond   http://www.prosuretybond.com/   Specializing in protecting government entities

Surety One, Inc.   https://suretyone.com/blog/internal-controls-fidelity-bond-must/

Nationwide   https://www.nationwide.com/   Fidelity Bonds for employee theft

Insureon   https://www.insureon.com/ Specializing in IT related employees

Case Law:
Avery Dennison Corp. v. Allendale Mutual Insurance Co.   *Fidelity Bonds and Intangible Property*

If your company has a policy of providing offenders with a second chance at employment, you should be aware that the department of labor established *The Federal Bonding Program* to provide fidelity bonds for at-risk job seekers. If you want to explore this further refer to www.bonds4jobs.com

Chapter 15 – Conclusion

15.0 Overview

You hear a lot about how important it is for a startup to prepare a *Business Plan*, but not always that much about an *Operations Plan*. An *Operations Plan* should be part of any well-conceived *Business Plan*. In other words as you grow what will your Org Chart look like, what skill sets will be required, what will it cost, and how will you draft a QMS (Quality Management System) or Operation Plan to support each level of growth. Depending on the nature of your company a plan for IT/security network operations will be needed as well.

If you're a small company, just getting started, as far as an Asset Management System (AMS) goes your goal should be to include the various processes displayed in the Flow Chart in Appendix-A ASAP, even if those processes are performed by a limited number of employees to begin with.

At the very least, you should employ *Property-of Labels (with unique asset identifiers)*, *Property Records (with placed in service dates, make, model, and serial number)*, an *Asset Tracker*, and *Asset Disposition Reports*. The longer you go without any order or an AMS in place, the greater chance of loss.

The other thing you will want to do at the outset is come up with a Document Control Record (DCR) system to properly catalog and identify your control forms. Refer to Chapter 3.

Obviously, the type of tracking technology and security to protect your assets will depend on the size and nature of your company or organization. At the very least most companies or government entities today employ video surveillance to protect their facilities and assets. This includes property numbers, location grids, and barcode labels to track their assets. Even if you're not ready for RFID technology or an integrated RFID-Video Surveillance system you would be wise plan ahead.

15.1 Preparing for System Upgrades

When you consider what a massive undertaking it would be to switch from legacy barcode labels to barcode labels with embedded RFID tags after operating for years, it may be advisable to consider going to barcode labels with embedded passive UHF RFID tags from the beginning – even if you aren't going to use the RFID tags anytime soon. The RFID tags are relatively inexpensive and when your enterprise, or government entity is ready to make the switch at least you won't have to go back and strip and replace all those property tags. A well thought out schema in advance for unique asset identifying *Property-of* labels is also advisable.

To prepare in advance for RFID will require that you purchase a desktop UHF RFID read-write device and software to write and test each UHF RFID tag as you create and apply them to each asset based on information on your Property Record. Refer to section (5.6).

15.2 Scaling an Asset Management System for Growth

It should be fairly easy to establish *Policies* or catalog *Data Collection Records* as you bring them online. However, it's a bit harder to draft and revise *Directives* to reflect various levels of growth, and task assignments as your organization is in a state of change, up or down. This includes not only updating Org charts, but job descriptions and reporting matrices as well as employee training curriculums. Without training and adequate skill set certifications, the controls required would be difficult to sustain, especially as employees come and go.

Asset Management System Flow Chart

Drafted by R.L. Bussiere

1 — Identify the Need ← Consider Cost Plus Maintenance

2 — Generate Requisition — Based on Policy

3 — Approval Process

Approve Release

Review Policy & Cost

4 — RFQ

5 — Bid / Contract Vendor Approval Process

Monitors Cash Flow Commitment

6 — Comptroller

7 — Purchase Order — A Purchase made directly with a Vendor or GPO

10 — Payment Voucher

9 — Copy AP

8 — Vendor Invoice — List Make, Model, Serial No. and Cost separately

11 — Receiving Warehouse — Vendor Ships Items with Pack List / Check Pack List Against Shipments

12 — Inspection

13 — Asset Record

Capitalized items Added to Depreciation & Amortization Detail Sheet

16 — Copy Accounting

15 — Place in Service

14 — Apply Property Tag — Barcode and/or RFID Tag

Mobile Assets Transferred to Tool Crib Pending Consignments

18 — Use Life

17 — Periodic Inventory

Use Map Grids or RFID Location System

Track condition of asset Includes Tool Crib Controls

Taken with a Tablet and Barcode Scanner / Typically by Department or Class

19 — Preventive Maintenance

20 — End of Life › Establish Value & Disposal Method

21 — Asset Disposition Report

22 — Property Reserve

23 — List & Prep for Auction or Donation

24 — Bill of Sale

25 — Proceeds to Corporation

26 — Compute Gain (Loss)

Prep for Disposal or Sale

Compute Gain Based on Book Value & Price

Procurement Process
Front End of Asset Management System

```
                        ┌──────────────────┐
                        │   Requisition    │
                        └──────────────────┘
                                 │
        Ref. Requisition                Ref. Requisition
              ┌──────┐                      ┌──────┐
              │ RFQ  │──────────────────────│ BID  │
              └──────┘                      └──────┘
                                              │
                                         ◇ Committee ◇
                                              │
   Release PO              ┌──────────────────┐
   From App'd Vendor List  │  Purchase Order  │◄────
   Ref. Vendor Quote       └──────────────────┘
                                 │
                                 ▼
                           ┌──────────────┐     Indentify Dcouments
                           │  Receiving   │     Daily Receiving Log
                           └──────────────┘     Inspect Goods
                                 │               Date Stamp Pack List
                                 │               Scan and File
                                 ▼
                           ┌──────────────┐     Apply Property Tag
                           │ Property Mgr │     Record Asset Details
                           └──────────────┘     Record Location
                                 │               Record First Service Date
                                 │               Track Asset
                                 │               Asset Disposition
                                 ▼
                        ┌──────────────────┐    Gather Documents
                        │ Accounts Payable │    Review Documents
                        └──────────────────┘    Prepare Pymt Voucher
                                                 Submit for Approval
                                                 Release Vendor Pymt
```

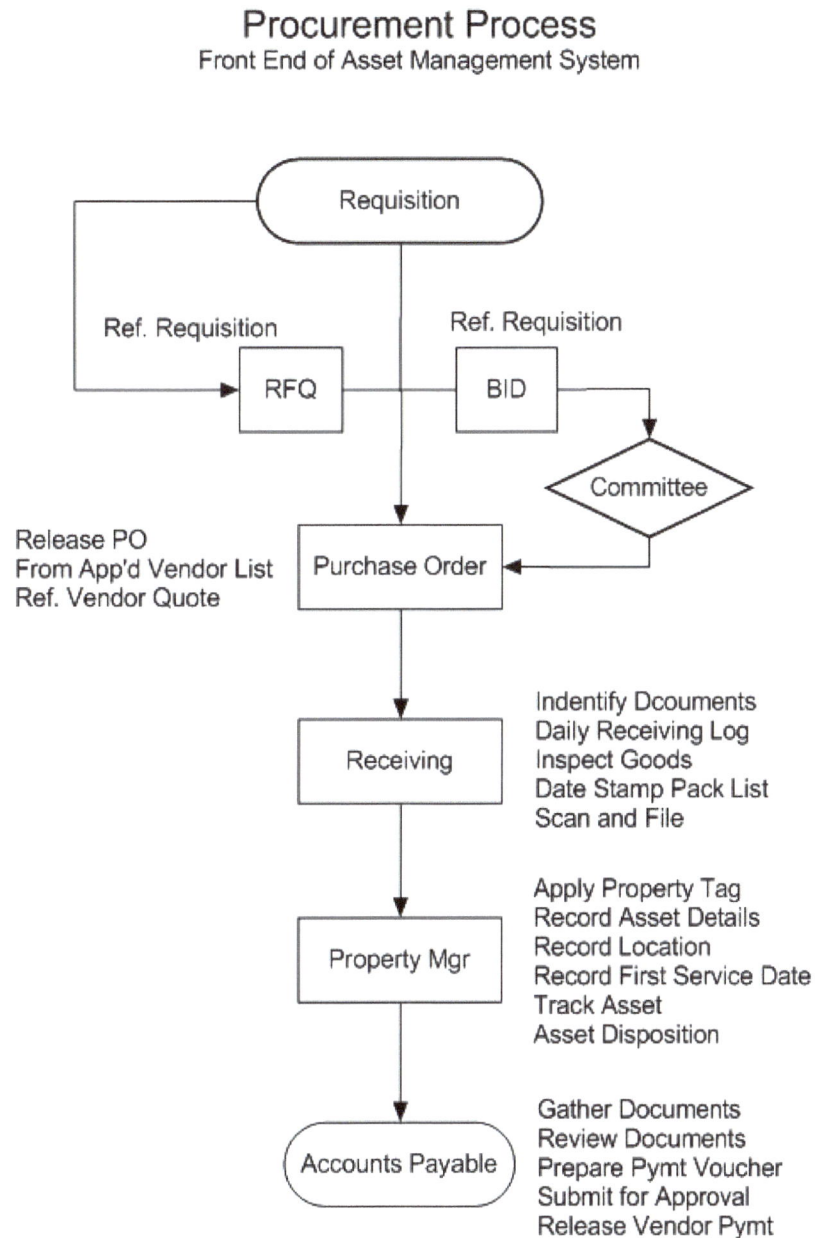

Routing Chart Participants

- Department Heads
- Purchasing Manager
- Receiving Manager
- Property Manager
- AP Clerk
- Accounting – calculate **Cost Basis** and capitalize or expense assets

Logo & Company Name
Address
Contact Information

ORDER REQUISITION
THIS IS NOT AN ORDER

Date Issued: 02/22/20
Date Approved:

E-Mail PDF

Request by

Employee No

Department
Sales

Job Title

Purpose or Intended Use

Interoffice Email

Acct No.   Vendor Contact: Ext

Vendor Name

Vendor Email

Open

○ Vendor on File

Needed in [1] days

Date Needed
02/23/20

NOTE:
Minimum inventory levels should be posted near the stock items in each department or the store room where supplies are kept to allow for normal delivery without the need to incur costs associated with expedited shipments.

List of Requisitioned Items

Item	Reorder No	Qty	Description of Requisitioned Item	ETA	Unit $	Ext. Total

[0] Total Items   Table Scrolls & Prints to Additional Pages

Total Net Cost $0.00
Freight Quote $0.00

Comments:

Approvals

Dept Head

Employee No

Purchasing Agent

Employee No

Final Approval by

Employee No

PO No

Purchase Orders

Dept Head Approval

Purchasing

Final Approval - Comptroller

Form No. 08-01-006-A

Page 1 of 1

Logo & Company Name
Address
Contact Information

VENDOR RECORD

VRN: | AA | – | 01 | – | 0001 |

Initials ———┘
Code - Vendor Type ———┘
Serial No ———┘

Our Contact Person: _____ EXT _____

Vendor Name: _____

Vendor Address: _____

Tel _____ Fax _____

Email
Fill _____ [Open]

Vendor Website
Fill _____ [Open]

Comments
Fill

Approval Date: _____
Credit Applied for Date: _____
Last Date Reseller Permit Sent _____
Credit Limit Issued

Credit
( ) Accepted   ( ) Rejected

Account No _____   Terms _____

Vendor Qualification
Vendor UBI/Tax No: _____
Survey Submission Date: _____
Date Rec'd & Qualified: _____
CDA Required? ( ) Yes ( ) No
If Yes, Date CDA Executed:: _____
CM/EMS Audit Required? ( ) Yes ( ) No
Last Audit Date: _____
Passed Audit? ( ) Yes ( ) No

[RFQ]
[Purchase Order]
[Routing Control]

Vendor Types   Identifies correct type for the purpose of soliciting bids

Code	Vendor Type	Code	Vendor Type	Code	Vendor Type
01	Components	13	Material Finishing	25	Reserve
02	Transformer Materials	14	Screen Printing	26	Reserve
03	Assembly Contractor	15	Stamping	27	Reserve
04	Wire Harnessing	16	Laminators	28	Reserve
05	PCB Maker	17	Water Jet Cutting	29	Reserve
06	Custom Transformers	18	Factory Supplies	30	Reserve
07	Machine Shop	19	Office/Engr. Supplies	31	Reserve
08	Sheet Metal Fabrication	20	Standards Documents	32	Reserve
09	Rapid Prototype	21	Starter Kit Repeat Items	33	Reserve
10	Molding	22	Sterilization	34	Reserve
11	Welding	23	Software	35	Reserve
12	Heat Treating	24	Computer Hardware	36	Reserve

Certifications
( ) ISO 9001 ( ) ISO 9002 ( ) Other
If either, is certification
( ) By Declaration ( ) By Agency

Agency _____

Approval Process

Check Active Reseller Permit every year.

Purchasing Agent _____   Accounting Manager _____

Note: Purchases or payments are not permitted without both signatures above.

Form No. 08-01-001-A

APPENDIX D

Logo & Company Name
Address
Contact Information

RFQ No: 00001

REQUEST FOR QUOTATION
THIS IS NOT AN ORDER

Our Contact Person: _____   EXT _____

Vendor Name: _____

Vendor Address: _____

Tel _____   Fax _____

Email _____   [Open]

Request Date: _____

Prints Attached: _____

Ship Via & Package for: _____

f.o.b. Point: _____

Account No: _____

Terms: _____

Buyer: _____

[E-Mail PDF]

FABRICATED ITEMS OR COMPONENTS

Item	LIN/Print No	Rev	Item Description	Qty	Make	Mfg Type	Standard Put-up	Last$/Un

| 0 | Total Items |

Table scrolls & prints to additional pages

Scheduling Requirement:

Calls for _____ Releases   Spread Over _____ months

Memo to Vendor
_____

Please include: Min. Release Qtys, Lead Times, and any NREs

Form No 08-01-004-A

Logo & Company Name
Address
Contact Information

REQUEST FOR QUOTATION
THIS IS NOT AN ORDER

Our Contact Person: _____ EXT _____

Vendor Name: _____

Vendor Address: _____

Tel _____ Fax _____

Email _____

Request Date: _____

Prints Attached: _____

Ship Via & Package for: _____

○ fob Point ○ Destin. Point

Account No: _____

Terms: _____

Buyer:

Scheduled Releases: _____

Scheduling Requirements

Sample Delivery Confirmation

Sample Qty _____ ○ None

Freight Tracking No. _____

A prepaid **Return Label** is included. Please return the samples in their original carton using the return label provided.

ASSEMBLY

Assembly LIN	Rev	Description	Qty	Last$/Un

Memo to EMS Contractor

NOTE: At minimum, all work should be in accordance with **ANSI (IPC-A-610F)** Electronic Assembly Standards. Refer to accompanying documentation for additional build standards. Build samples are provided for each order with kits as well as any required consigned tools from our tool crib. Kits are supplied in tie-wrapped sealed tubo cases with serial numbers - referenced on accompanied **Material Transfer Receipts**. Typically, passive components are packed by type in barcode labeled zipper bags and ICs are delivered in rails. SMDs are delivered on individually packed tape strips or on reels.

List of Build Documents

Item	Doc/LIN/PCN	ECO/Rev	Document Description

0 Total Documents

List of Consigned Tools

Item	Tag No.	Tool

Table Scrolls

0 Total Tools

Form No 08-01-004-A

Please include: Min. Release Qtys, Lead Times, and any NREs

Logo & ACME Corporation
Address
Contact Information

UBI No.

No. JD-00001

PURCHASE ORDER

Date: 12/12/19

Requisition No.		○ Vendor ○ GPO ○ Host	Our Account: No	
Vendor No.		Ext	Terms	

Vendor Contact:

Email: [ ] Open

Receiving Dock: ● A ○ B ○ C   [E-Mail PDF]

Vendor or GPO	Ship to Instructions
	Receiving Dock ACME Corporation 1234-100th Ave. North Seattle, WA 98004

Tel: [ ] Fax: [ ]

Tel Notification (If Required): [ ]

Please mark all cartons with our reference P.O. Number

Ref. Quote	Ref. WO / Project No.	Tax	Freight Term (Fob Destin)	Ship Via
		Yes		

○ Material ○ Supply Items ● Equipment   Please use separate for each of these three categories

FRT PPD

Item	Type No.	Description	Release	Qty	Unit $	Ext. Total
1	PL-098456	Copier	1/10/20	1	$3,500.00	$3,500.00

1	Total Items Ordered - Per Page	Total Net Amount	$3,500.00

Special Instructions

Each equipment line item on your invoice/packing list must be listed separately by make, model, serial number, and net cost as well as ship weight in lbs for each line item plus the total cost of freight and any sales tax.

Purchasing Agent

Name & Title:

Additional Terms & Conditions

Authorization Signature

Name & Title:

Suppliers of raw materials and components - please include lot codes, RoHS Compliance Statement, and certificate(s) of conformity.

CONFIRMING COPY

Form No 08-03-008-A

93

Page 1 of 1

Daily Receiving Log

Date Rec'd	Pack List No Via Barcode	Vendor	Items Rec'd	Items BO	Asset Items	PO No From Pack List	Tracking No. Via Barcode	Cartons	Weight lbs	Recorded By Via Barcode
11/12/19										

To enter today's date - right click go to Insert/Date   Asset Items - Defined as operating equipment, devices, or instruments - not supply or disposal items   Table Scrolls & Prints to Additional Pages

Logo & Company Name
Address
Contact Information

Control No.   000001

AP CHECK VOUCHER

Date: 2/16/2020

Requisition		PO No		Batch No
00004	Open Record		Open Record	2019-00001

Vendor No		Pack List (1)		Debit GL Acct No 5055
	Open Record	000100	Open Record	

RFQ		Vendor Invoice		Daily Rec'g Log
	Open Record		Open Record	

BID No		Invoice Amount
	Open Record	

* AP Clerk

Approved by

(1) **Open Record** only works if Pack List is received, stamped, and scanned to PDF File then stored in the server. Use **Show List** for others.

Form No   05-01-024-A

NOTE: Using Formdocs*, the FAB Script below is embedded in the OPEN RECORD button for the vendor Pack List. It's identified by the Pack List number entered in the Data Field to the left of the button. The "URL=" line of code under the path statement to display a PDF copy of the Pack List is an example of the syntax to open the Requisition.fdd or any other (.fdd) recordset file. Once in the (.fdd) recordset, click SHOW LIST in the upper right hand corner in Formdocs* and a list of serial numbers for eform records will appear in that record set. Just click on the number appearing in the Data Field on the proceeding AP Check Voucher to open that specific record. Of course, you will need to change the path statements for the location of your files.

```
Private Sub Find Pack List Click ()
Dim URL As String

' Displays the target document in its own application.
' Replace the sample URL with your own URL in the form of
' file://path\filename.extension.

        On Error Goto Bad

        URL = "file://f:\FORMS\08-Purchasing\PDF Archives\Pack Lists\" & Thisform.fields("Pack_List").value & ".pdf"
'       URL = "file://f:\FORMS\08-Purchasing\Requisition.fdd"
'       URL = InputBox("Enter a pathname for the document to display and click OK.", "Open Local Document", URL)
        If (0 = Len(URL)) Then
                Exit Sub
        End If

        Application.Hyperlink(URL)
        Exit Sub

Bad:    MsgBox("Hyperlink Failed: " & Error(), 16)


End Sub
```

Logo & Company Name

Address
Contact Information

AP Check List

Payment Date	2019-12-08		GL Acct	5055	Group	Trade Debt

Right Click to Insert System Date

AP VOUCHERS

No.	Vendor No	Payee	Invoice	Ref PO	Check No	Amount

0	Table scrolls and prints to additional pages	Total for all pages	$0.00

Note: Gather and review the Vendor Invoice, stamped Pack List, and reference PO to verify each payment above using your read-only access to PO records.

AP Clerk _____   Approved by _____

Form No   05-02016-A

Page 1 of 1

Logo & Company Name
Address
Contact Information

Control No   00001
Cost Basis Calculator
Asset Management Record

Directive

Invoice Date	12/04/19
Vendor	Acme
Invoice No	008345

Total Invoice Net Amt	7,235.00
Total Shipping Cost	$204.00
Total Ship Weight	75.00 lbs
Total Sales Tax	$773.66

Property No	Description	Ship Weight (lbs)	Percent	Ship'g Cost	Net Cost	Tax %	Line Item Tax	Other Cost	Total Cost Basis
D-03-00003	PC Tower	45.00	60.00%	$122.40	5,632.00	77.84%	$602.25	$993.00	$7,349.65
E-03-00004	Computer Monitor	24.00	32.00%	$65.28	1,451.00	20.06%	$155.16		$1,671.44
E-03-00005	Keyboard	5.00	6.67%	$13.60	103.00	1.42%	$11.01		$127.61
E-03-00006	Mouse	1.00	1.33%	$2.72	49.00	0.68%	$5.24		$56.96
			0.00%	$0.00		0.00%	$0.00		$0.00
			0.00%	$0.00		0.00%	$0.00		$0.00
			0.00%	$0.00		0.00%	$0.00		$0.00
			0.00%	$0.00		0.00%	$0.00		$0.00
			0.00%	$0.00		0.00%	$0.00		$0.00
		75.00	100.00%	$204.00	$7,235.00	100.00%	$773.66		

Table Scrolls

Property No	D-03-00003			
Other Cost Basis	Invoice No	Other Cost		
Electrical Service		$436.00		
Installation		$212.00		
Local Inspection Sticker		$75.00		
Support Service Contract		$270.00		
Table Scrolls		$993.00		

Property No				
Other Cost Basis	Invoice No	Other Cost		
Table Scrolls		$0.00		

Property No				
Other Cost Basis	Invoice No	Other Cost		
Table Scrolls		$0.00		

APPENDIX J

97

Logo & Corporate Name
Contact Info

Property Record   E - 02-00003

Directive	Video		Property Tag

TYPE
D - Depreciate
A - Amortized
E - Expensed

CLASS
02-Computers Peripherals ▼

Date Placed In Service [ ]

Requisition No [ ]   **Order Date** [ ]   **PO No** [ ]

Vendor No [ ]   **Vendor** [ ]   **Invoice No** [ ]

Vendor Phone No [ ]   **Vendor Email** [ ]

Rec'd [ ]   **Ship lbs** [ ]   **Net Cost** [ ]   **Sales Tax** [ ]

Warranty Period [ ] mos   **Age** [ ] yrs

Service Agmt [ ]   [Agmt]   **Subscription Fee** [ ]

Map Grid Location [ ]   **Dept** [ ]   **Section** [ ]

Residual
◯ Leased ◯ Option to Buy [ ]

Cost Basis [ ]   **IRS Class** [ ]   **Life/Yrs** [ ]   **Salvage Value** [ ]

◯ Sec. 179   Safe Harbor Amt $5,000.00

Asset ◯ Tangible ◯ Intangible

Cost Recovery ◯ DDB ◯ Striaght Line ◯ Expensed

Bid ◯ Yes ◯ No   Group Purchase ◯ Yes ◯ No

Qualifying Documents - include copy of invoice and how warranty is conveyed

Doc No.	Title	File Location

Co-op Purchase ◯ Yes ◯ No   Use Map Grid Code for Shared Use Location

Aspect Ratio: 16:9

Property Description
Bar Code/ RFID Scanner

Make [ ]   **Model** [ ]

Serial No [ ]

RFID - PC [ ]

GPS Command Set File - Tag ID [ ]

Placement ◯ Stationary ◯ Mobile

Host Entity [ ]

Number of Participants [ ]

[Documents]   Scrolling Table

Receiving Manager Date [ ]   **Dept Head** Placement Date [ ]   **Accounting** Date [ ]

[Export]   [Next Page >]

FORM No./ Rev. 08-03-025-A   PART 1   98   Page 1 of 2

Logo & Corporate Name
Contact Info

Property Description

Bar Code/ RFID Scanner

Make   Model

Map Grid Location Dept   Section

Serial No

List of Combination Accessories:

Item	Reorder No.	Brand	Description	Qty	Cost	Extended Life/mos

| | Total Accessory Items |

Table Scrolls

Preventative Maintenance Events:

Service Manual on F   ◯ Yes ◯ No   File by Property No.

Event	Date	Employee No	PCN	PM Record	Service Preformed

| 0 | Total Events |

Table Scrolls

NOTE:
File PCN (Process Control No. Document) with Service Manual. All
PM event records must be signed and include Employee No...

Property Reserve Trxf   Date

Service Life Upon Trxf [   ] Yrs

< Prev Page

Preventative Maintenance Label – a record of PM events applied to the asset itself.   See Property Record
Created in DYMO LabelWriter*   Adhesive Label DYMO # 99019   2-5/16" x 7-1/2"

```
      Maintenance Record
       PCN: 01-00043-A

   DATE      Tech      Rev
```

Note: The PCN (Process Control Number) is the directive issued for the PM event required for this asset. It can be changed in real time in DYMO LabelWriter before printing.

Company Name
Depreciation and Amortization Detail

Report Date: 12/31/29   Save each FYE detail sheet to a separate xls or pdf file for reference

Based on: MACRS Table Appendix A-1- IRS Publication 946

Asset No.	Date Placed in Service	Method IRC Sec.	Life (Yrs)	Rate %	First Period Mos	Period Full	Cost or Other Basis	Salvage Value	Adjusted Basis	Accumulated Depre/Amort	Current Year Deduction	Net of Depre/Amort
OFFICE EQUIPMENT (MACRS Table - Class 00.11)								0%		Make	Model	SN
C-01-00001 Desk										Hon	HP3262	19-0023456
	01/01/19	DDB	7.00	28.57	11.00	8.00	$500.00	$0.00	$0.00	$500.00	$0.00	$0.00
C-01-00002 Desk										Hon	HP3262	19-0023457
	01/01/19	DDB	7.00		11.00	8.00	$500.00	$0.00	$0.00	$500.00	$0.00	$0.00
C-01-00003 Desk										Hon	HP3262	19-0023458
	01/01/19	DDB	7.00		11.00	8.00	$1,500.00	$0.00	$0.00	$1,500.00	$0.00	$0.00
C-01-00003 Optional Desk Accessory												
	01/01/19	DDB	7.00		11.00	8.00			$1,000.00	$1,000.00	$0.00	$0.00
TOTAL OFFICE EQUIPMENT							$2,500.00	$0.00	$0.00	$2,500.00	$0.00	($0.00)
COMPUTER EQUIPMENT (MACRS Table - Class 00.12)								0%		Make	Model	SN
C-02-00004 PC - Tower										IBM	X7	19-0023456
	01/01/19	DDB	5.00	40.00		6.00	$2,300.00	$0.00	$0.00	$2,300.00	$132.48	$0.00
C-02-00005 PC - Tower										IBM	X7	19-0023457
	01/01/19	DDB	5.00			6.00	$1,500.00	$0.00	$0.00	$1,500.00	$86.40	$0.00
C-02-0006 PC - Tower												19-0023458
	01/01/19	DDB	5.00			6.00	$1,200.00	$0.00	$0.00	$1,200.00	$69.12	$0.00
TOTAL COMPUTER EQUIPMENT							$5,000.00	$0.00	$0.00	$5,000.00	$288.00	$0.00
LAB EQUIPMENT (MACRS Table - Class 35.0)								0%		Make	Model	SN
C-03-00007 DVM										Fluke	87	19-0023456
	01/01/19	DDB	7.00			8.00	$650.00	$0.00	$0.00	$650.00	$0.00	$0.00
C-03-00008 Scope										Tektronix	2230	19-0023457
	01/01/19	DDB	7.00			8.00	$2,300.00	$0.00	$0.00	$2,300.00	$0.00	$0.00
C-03-00009 Power Supply										HP	100	19-0023458
	01/01/19	DDB	7.00			8.00	$1,000.00	$0.00	$0.00	$1,000.00	$0.00	$0.00
TOTAL LAB EQUIPMENT							$3,950.00	$0.00	$0.00	$3,950.00	$0.00	($0.00)

PLANT EQUIPMENT (MACRS Table - Class 35.0)

ID	Description	Date	Method			Cost	%			Make	Model		SN	
C-04-00010	Lathe - Toolroom							0%		Hardinge	HLVH			
		01/01/19	DDB	7.00	8.00	$17,500.00		$0.00	$17,500.00	$0.00	$0.00	$0.00	19-0023456	$0.00
C-04-00011	Drill Press									Delta	2230			
		01/01/19	DDB	7.00	8.00	$2,300.00		$0.00	$2,300.00	$0.00	$0.00	$0.00	19-0023457	$0.00
C-04-00012	Milling Machine									Bridgeport	X70			
		01/01/19	DDB	7.00	8.00	$10,000.00		$0.00	$10,000.00	$0.00	$0.00	$0.00	19-0023458	$0.00
TOTAL PLANT EQUIPMENT						**$29,800.00**		**$0.00**	**$29,800.00**	**$29,800.00**	**$0.00**	**$0.00**		**$0.00**

Production Tooling (MACRS Table - Class 34.01)

ID	Description	Date	Method			Cost	%			Make	Model		SN	
C-04-00010	Injection Mold							0%						
		01/01/19	DDB	3.00	4.00	$17,500.00		$0.00	$17,500.00	$17,500.00	$0.00	$0.00	19-0023456	$0.00
C-04-00011	Aluminum Vacuum Forming Die													
		01/01/19	DDB	3.00	4.00	$2,300.00		$0.00	$2,300.00	$2,300.00	$0.00	$0.00	19-0023457	$0.00
C-04-00012	Drill Jig													
		01/01/19	DDB	3.00	4.00	$10,000.00		$0.00	$10,000.00	$10,000.00	$0.00	$0.00	19-0023458	$0.00
TOTAL TOOLING						**$29,800.00**		**$0.00**	**$29,800.00**	**$29,800.00**	**($0.00)**	**$0.00**		**$0.00**

SOFTWARE — IRS Section 179/197

ID	Description	Date	Method	SLN	#	Cost	%			Make	Model		SN	
C-05-00013	Windows OS - W7							0%		MS	W7			
		01/01/19	SL	36	36	$540.00		$0.00	$540.00	$540.00	$0.00	$0.00	19-0023456	$0.00
C-05-00014	MS Office									MS	2010			
		01/01/19	SL	36	36	$625.00		$0.00	$625.00	$625.00	$0.00	$0.00	19-0023457	$0.00
C-05-00015	SolidWorks									SW	2019			
		01/01/19	SL	36	36	$2,000.00		$0.00	$2,000.00	$2,000.00	$0.00	$0.00	19-0023458	$0.00
TOTAL SOFTWARE						**$3,165.00**		**$0.00**	**$3,165.00**	**$3,165.00**	**$0.00**	**$0.00**		**$0.00**

TRADEMARKS — Product TMs Only (14 yrs)

ID	Description	Date	Method	SLN	#	Cost	%			Make	Model		SN	
C-06-00016	Dynastrode							0%						
		01/01/19	SL	168	131	$1,750.00		$0.00	$1,364.58	$1,364.58	$125.00	$385.42	19-0023456	$0.00
C-06-00017	Digi-DAC													
		01/01/19	SL	168	131	$2,450.00		$0.00	$1,910.42	$1,910.42	$175.00	$539.58	19-0023457	$0.00
C-06-00018	C-SW													
		01/01/19	SL	168	131	$5,000.00		$0.00	$3,898.81	$3,898.81	$357.14	$1,101.19	19-0023458	$0.00
TOTAL TRADEMARKS						**$9,200.00**		**$0.00**	**$7,173.81**	**$7,173.81**	**$657.14**	**$2,026.19**		**$0.00**

PATENTS

ID	Description	Date	Method	Useful Life (10 yrs)	#			0%		SN		0%
C-07-00019	Plasma Discharge Switch	01/01/19	SL	120	#	$6,700.00	$0.00	$0.00	$6,700.00	19-0023456	$55.83	$0.00
C-07-00020	UP/SN Prescaler	01/01/19	SL	120	#	$4,500.00	$0.00	$0.00	$4,500.00	19-0023457	$37.50	$0.00
C-07-00021	BCD-Binary Converter	01/01/19	SL	120	#	$7,200.00	$0.00	$0.00	$7,200.00	19-0023458	$60.00	$0.00
TOTAL PATENTS - (Economic Life)						$18,400.00	$0.00	$0.00	$18,400.00		$153.33	$0.00

COPYRIGHTS

ID	Description	Date	Method	Useful Life (10 yrs)	#			0%		SN		0%
C-08-00022	Principles of Electrosurgery	01/01/19	SL	120	#	$5,000.00	$0.00	$0.00	$5,000.00	19-0023456	$41.67	$0.00
C-08-00023	Guide to Performance & Safety Testing	01/01/19	SL	120	#	$4,500.00	$0.00	$0.00	$4,500.00	19-0023457	$37.50	$0.00
C-08-00024	Line Numbering Schemes & Related Practices in Manufacturing	01/01/19	SL	120	#	$15,000.00	$0.00	$0.00	$15,000.00	19-0023458	$125.00	$0.00
TOTAL COPYRIGHTS						$24,500.00	$0.00	$0.00	$24,500.00		$204.17	$0.00

CONTRACT RIGHTS

ID	Description	Date	Method	Term	#			0%		SN		0%
C-09-00025]	Patent Assignment	01/01/19	SL	120	#	$45,000.00	$0.00	$0.00	$45,000.00	19-0023456	$375.00	$0.00
C-09-00026	Licensing Agreement	01/01/19	SL	60	#	$25,000.00	$0.00	$0.00	$25,000.00	19-0023457	$0.00	$0.00
C-09-00027	Licensing Agreement	01/01/19	SL	60	#	$15,000.00	$0.00	$0.00	$15,000.00	19-0023458	$0.00	$0.00
TOTAL CONTRACTS - Assignments Based on Economic Life						$85,000.00	$0.00	$0.00	$85,000.00		$375.00	$0.00

Intangibles Based on IRS Section 197

Notes:

=DDB($Cost,SalvageValue,Life,n)   (When Salvage is 10% or more)

Tangible Assets - DDB MACRS IRS Table by Class

Intangible Assets - SLN Amortization (Based on useful life)

Trademarks - Amortized product related trademarks only - not corporation trade/mark name.

For First Year Recovery - Use Half Year Convention for Fourth Quarter Purchases (Placement) - Use Mid Quarter Convention

This spreadsheet does not include Sec 179 Bonus Depreciation - Refer to current IRS code

Company Name

	No.	Period	Report Name
Report Date :	0808004A	2019-FYE	List of Pending Sales Orders
Report Date :	11/05/19	Items This Report	Lost Assets
Class :	08	2	1
Recordset :	F:\Forms\08>Assets\Asset Tracker.fdd		
Source Date :	F:\Forms\08>Assets\Excel\Data Files\0808004.csv		
Report File :	F:\Forms\08>Assets\Excel\Reports\0808004-08	2019-FYE.xlsx	
Employee :	John Doe		

Save File

								Condition of Asset			Sch.					
Property No	Record	Location	Class	Description	Make	MN	SN	Good	Fair	Poor	PM	Lost	Comment	Audit	Time Stamped
E-01-00001	00001	SW-01-05-07	8	PC Tower	IBM	100	9875456832	T			T		Windows 10 OS	T	11/5/19 6:09 PM
D-02-00002	00002	SW-02-05-04	8	Mill	Bridgeport	200	9234376129					T	Cam Software	T	11/5/19 6:24 PM

VBA – embedded in the Excel "Asset Report" (see Appendix N)
Created in Excel (Developer) Design Mode*

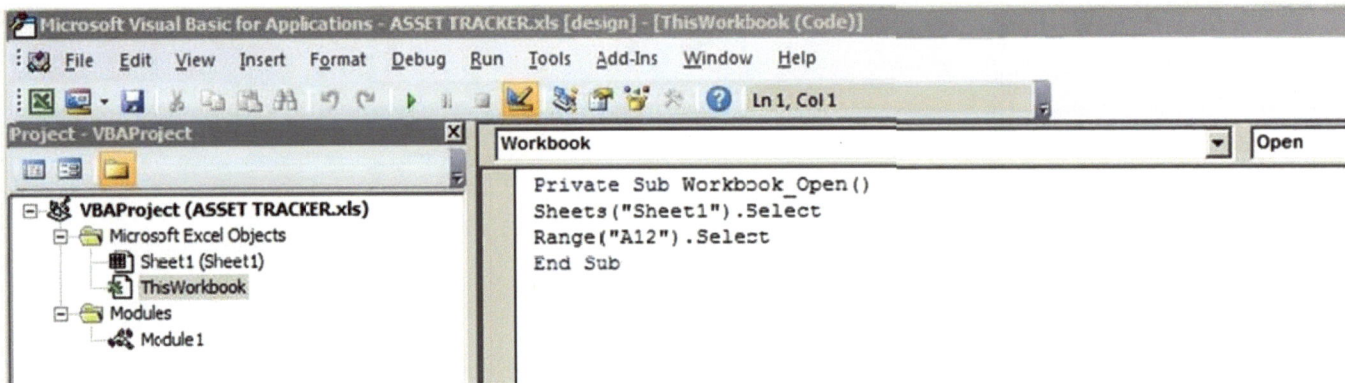

```
Microsoft Visual Basic for Applications - ASSET TRACKER.xls [design] - [ThisWorkbook (Code)]
File  Edit  View  Insert  Format  Debug  Run  Tools  Add-Ins  Window  Help
                                                            Ln 1, Col 1

Project - VBAProject                      Workbook                    Open

VBAProject (ASSET TRACKER.xls)        Private Sub Workbook_Open()
  Microsoft Excel Objects               Sheets("Sheet1").Select
    Sheet1 (Sheet1)                     Range("A12").Select
    ThisWorkbook                        End Sub
  Modules
    Module1
```

08-Assets
  08-Directives
  Data Files
  Excel Files
    Masters
    Reports
  PDF Files
  Recordsets

Simple File Storage Schema for these examples

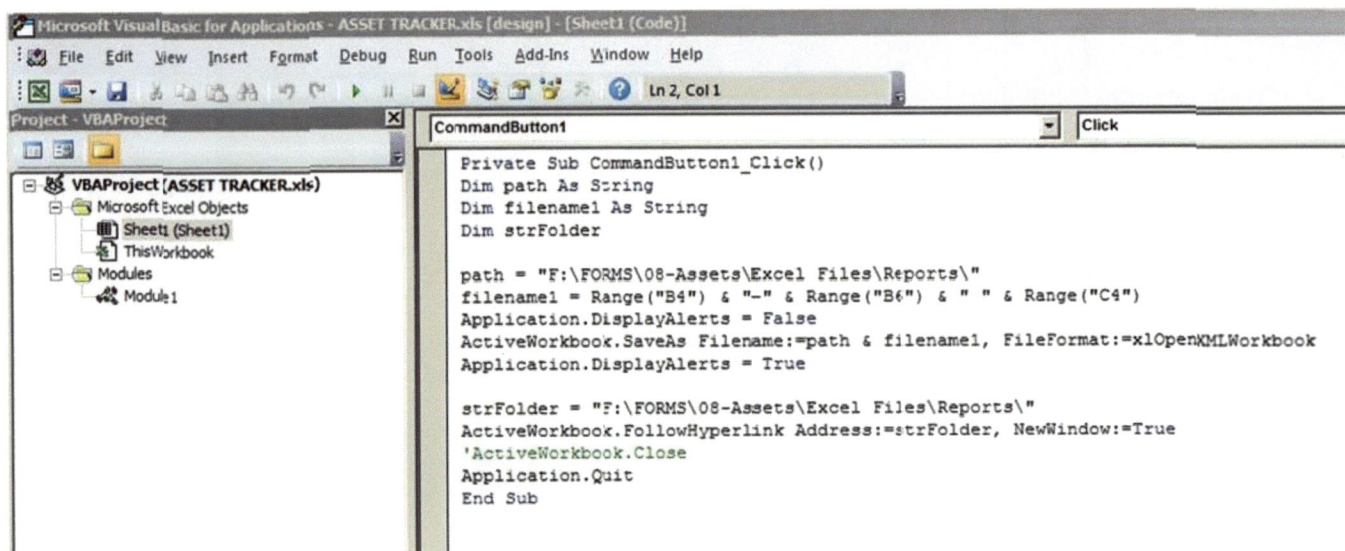

```
Microsoft Visual Basic for Applications - ASSET TRACKER.xls [design] - [Sheet1 (Code)]
File  Edit  View  Insert  Format  Debug  Run  Tools  Add-Ins  Window  Help
                                                            Ln 2, Col 1

Project - VBAProject                      CommandButton1                Click

VBAProject (ASSET TRACKER.xls)        Private Sub CommandButton1_Click()
  Microsoft Excel Objects               Dim path As String
    Sheet1 (Sheet1)                     Dim filename1 As String
    ThisWorkbook                        Dim strFolder
  Modules
    Module1                             path = "F:\FORMS\08-Assets\Excel Files\Reports\"
                                        filename1 = Range("B4") & "-" & Range("B6") & " " & Range("C4")
                                        Application.DisplayAlerts = False
                                        ActiveWorkbook.SaveAs Filename:=path & filename1, FileFormat:=xlOpenXMLWorkbook
                                        Application.DisplayAlerts = True

                                        strFolder = "F:\FORMS\08-Assets\Excel Files\Reports\"
                                        ActiveWorkbook.FollowHyperlink Address:=strFolder, NewWindow:=True
                                        'ActiveWorkbook.Close
                                        Application.Quit
                                        End Sub
```

Note: Uses a mobile Asset Tracker to gather inventory/audit data. Then that data is transferred to an Assets Report in Excel similar to the one displayed in Appendix N for management review. The top VBA/Macros automatically highlights the first cell in the data range to import data either via the Data Import ribbon or copy and paste it fro the data file. The lower Macro displayed automatically picks specific cell values indicated in the script to name the file and then runs the Command Save As button to generate the report file in the correct Reports Folder.

Asset Track r - for use with mobile tablet
Created in Formdocs*

Asset Tracker

PROPERTY NO.

E-01-00001

RECORD

00001

MAP GRID - Location

SW-01-05-07

CLASS

08

DESCRIPTION

PC Tower

MAKE

IBM

MN

100

SN

9873456832

CONDITION

◉ Good   ○ Fair   ○ Poor

◉ Sch. PM   ○ Asset Lost

COMMENT

Windows 10 OS

DATE TIME STAMP

Audit ◉   11/5/2019 6:09:01 PM

SAVE THEN NEXT RECORD
FORM NO. 08-03-004-A

Export

Note: The employee tasked with taking inventory should be entered on the spreadsheet or database where the batch record data is exported. Wipe the .csv data columns and line items on the temporary Excel spreadsheet to the one you properly formatted for your final report(s) using CTRL-C / CTRL-V. Those reports can be by department , map grid location, class, type, or group whether inventory is taken by one or more employees. Refer to the schema for the Property No. or the Map Grid. Use Formdocs* SEARCH to collect only those records from the master Property recordset you need for each batch report from the master database using the path location in the ODBC/DSN file and to automatically prefill the **Asset Tracker** above.   Once you fill the Property No Field by (1) scanning the barcoded tag (using Formdocs* Autofill) or (2) via NFC tag, you should only need to fill the variable data fields from CONDITION on down. We used a Windows 10 Vanquisher 8-Inch Industrial Tablet MN: SV-86(H) - with NFC capability. Use Bluetooth with wireless barcode scanner or corded type.

Programmer	Example	Dept - Sec	
Ron Bussiere	Export to CSV file	08-03	Rev Date: 10/31/19

Describe Automation Function   ● Action Button   ○ Template Properties   ○ Page Properties   ○ Field Properties

EXPORT Action Button FAB script. Exports recordset data to csv file in Excel. This FAB script names the Data file with the source recordset Form No. and Rev. Code. Based on the script below after the Export button saves the data to a .csv file in the Data Folder a dialog box pops up and instructs the user where to retrieve the comma delimited data. Note: A macro in the Excel Read Only (Master File) opens in the first data range cell. Once the data is imported into the Excel Master it can all be saved to a Report File in a Reports Folder. That final report file uses a macro to name, date, and locate the report file.

FAB Script

○ Calculation

Programmable Event

Click

```
Private Sub BTN_EXPORT_Click ()
Dim sPathName As String
Dim FN As String

' Exports as CSV all records in the current recordset.
' Creates a file having the same name as the form with a ".csv" extension
' Change the pathname to meet your own needs.

        On Error Goto Bad
        If False = Thisform.Saved Then
                MsgBox ("Please 'Save' the file before exporting!", 16)
                Exit Sub
        End If

        ' Note: you can specify a path and filename two (2) different ways:
        ' 1. Program a hardcoded path & filename.
        ' 2. Prompt using Application.GetSaveAsFileName().
        ' prompt user to select the output filename:

        sPathName = "F:\FORMS\08-Assets\Data Files\" & "0803004A" & ".csv"
        ' sPathName = GetSaveAsFileName ("CSV Files,*.CSV", 1, "Export Recordset to CSV", sPathName)
        If Len (sPathName) <= 0 Then
        Exit Sub
        End If

        FN="Property_Tag,Record_No,Location,Class,Description,Make,MN,Product_SN,Good,Fair,Poor,PM,Missing,Comment,Audit,Stamp"

        Thisform.Export (sPathName, fdFormatText, fdRangeRecordSet, FN, True, ",")
        MsgBox ("To view the exported data, open the data folder using a shortcut icon on your desktop. Use CTRL-C to copy the data fields only from the data
file and  CTRL-V to paste that data to a preformatted Excel Worksheet. The filename is the recordset Form No: " & sPathName, 64)
        Exit Sub

Bad:
        MsgBox("CSV Export Failed: " & Error(), 16)
End Sub
```

Customer Email

Text Field Scrolls & Prints to Additional Page(s)

Logo & Company Name
Address
Contact Information

Receipt **No.** 00001

TOOL CRIB RECEIPT

Property No   05-0002

Crib Rack & Bin Location

Property No.

Description of Property   MN   SN

Tool Kit Accessories - bits, set keys, dies, batteries, cases, etc.

Item	Reorder No	Mfgr Type	Qty	Description of Accessory

0   Total Accessories   Table Scrolls

Assignment

Complete all information above this line in advance.

Employee No.

● Days   ○ Swing   ○ Grave Yard   Training Cert.

Employee No.   Employee Name: Department   Job Title
09-0001

WO No.   LIN Assembly   Rev   Assembly Description   Build Qty   Staging Area Used

IN / OUT Tracking

Instructions: All property released from tool crib to be returned immediately upon completion of job.

Date   Time   Date   Time

● Released   09/11/17   13:40   ○ Returned

Stores / Tool Crib Mgr.   Stores / Tool Crib Mgr.

Property Inspection

If so, list here by SN or Item Number

○ Tool or Accessories Missing

○ Tool or Accessories Need Replacement

○ Tool or Accessories Need Repair

○ Tool or Accessories Need Calibration

○ Purchasing Notified of Requirements

Note: Maintain any battery chargers in tool crib and charge prior to release.

Requisition No.   Stores / Tool Crib Mgr.

Form No   08-03-003-A

108

Page 1 of 1

Logo & Company Name
Address
Contact Information

Control No **0100**

HR - Consigned Assets Record

Employee's Name	Job Title	Assigned WS	Original Issuance Date	12/12/17

Revision

Department	Department Head	Supervisor	Revision Date

Instructions: *When company assets are consigned to an employee complete this form and generate a copy, including any revisions thereof.*

List of Consigned Items - check and identify all that apply

☐ Employee ID Badge

Employee ID

Badge Hardware - Holder, Lanyard, clips

☐ Building Key

Key No.

Keys to what area of the building

☐ Tool Crib Key

Key No.

Keys to what Crib or Drawer No

☐ Business Cards

Qty

☐ Uniform(s)   Qty   Size

☐ Pager

Property Tag   Make   MN   SN   Pager No

☐ Cell Phone

Property Tag   Make   MN   SN   Phone No

Plan Provider   Acct No   Service Provider Email Contact

☐ Laptop

Property Tag   Make   MN   SN   Operating System

Email - Laptop Contact   Address formatted per company protocol

☐ Vehicle & Key

Property Tag   Make   MN   VIN No   License No

Current Mileage   Last Service Date   12/12/17   Leasing Agency   Email Contact

☐ Gas Credit Card

Company   Acct/Card No   Date Expires $ Limit   Email Contact

☐ Other Items

List of Tools Consigned - as a general rule tools are not allowed to leave the company facilities unless they are part of a field service kit

Item	Property Tag	Description	MN	SN

0	Total Items	Scrolling Table

NOTE: Should you leave our company you will need to return these items before your Exit Interview, in order to ensure prompt payment of any remaining compensation. If you should lose or damage property entrusted to you, you are required to report it within 3 days of loss.

Employee Signature   Date

Form No   04-01-007-A   Print

Acknowledging delivery of items above

Page 1 of 1

Logo & Company Name
Address
Contact Information

Control No 0001

HR - Returned Assets Receipt

Employee's Name	Job Title	Assigned WS	Original Issuance Date	05/21/19

Revision

Department	Department Head	Supervisor	Revision Date

Instructions: **When company assets are consigned to an employee complete this form and generate a copy, including any revisions thereof.**

List of Consigned Items - check and identify all that apply

☐ Employee ID Badge

Employee ID | Badge Hardware - Holder, Lanyard, clips

☐ Building Key

Key No. | Keys to what area of the building

☐ Tool Crib Key

Key No. | Keys to what Crib or Drawer No

☐ Business Cards

Qty | ☐ Uniform(s) | Qty | Size

☐ Pager

Property Tag | Make | MN | SN | Pager No

☐ Cell Phone

Property Tag | Make | MN | SN | Phone No

Plan Provider | Acct No | Service Provider Email Contact

☐ Laptop

Property Tag | Make | MN | SN | Operating System

Email - Laptop Contact | Address formatted per company protocol

☐ Vehicle & Key

Property Tag | Make | MN | VIN No | License No

Current Mileage | Last Service Date 05/21/19 | Leasing Agency | Email Contact

☐ Gas Credit Card

Company | Acct/Card No | Date Expires | $ Limit | Email Contact

☐ Other Item

List of Tools Consigned - as a general rule tools are not allowed to leave the company facilities unless they are part of a field service kit

Item	Property Tag	Description	MN	SN

0	Total Items	Scrolling Table

NOTE: Should you leave our company you will need to return these items before your Exit Interview, in order to ensure prompt payment of any remaining compensation. If you should lose or damage property entrusted to you, you are required to report it within 3 days of loss.

Employer Signature | Date

Acknowledging delivery of items above

Form No | Print

Logo & Corporate Name
Contact Info

ASSET DISPOSITION REPORT

Property No. **E-01-00001**

[Directive] [Video]

Dept [   ]

Map Grid Location [   ]

In Service [   ] Yrs.

Report Date [   ]

○ Capitalized ○ Expensed

Item Description [   ] Make [   ] MN [   ] SN [   ]

Status: ○ Gone Missing ○ Needs Repair ○ End of Useful Life ○ Found After Reported Missing

Was item missing ever tracked? ○ Yes ○ No   If Yes, last report date: [   ]   Last PM date: [   ]

Describe status, condition or service required   Warranty Remaining? ○ Yes ○ No   Refer to Asset Tracker

[   ]

Describe service last performed   Refer to Property Record

[   ]

Original Purchase Data
○ Purchased ○ Consignment ○ Leased

PO Date [   ] PO No [   ] Vendor [   ] Vendor Invoice [   ] Date Rec'd [   ] Net Amt [   ]

Date Placed in Service [   ]   Leased - Option to Buy ○ Yes ○ No   Residual Amt [   ]

○ Lease Item Purchased for Title   Lease term in months [   ]   Lease Pymt [   ]

Property Reserve Record

Transfer Date [   ]

If Donated or Scrapped

Name of Business who took possession [   ]

Scheduled for: ○ Repair ○ Sale ○ Auction ○ Donation ○ Scrap

Date [   ]   Receipt No. [   ]

○ Return to Service - after repair   ○ Returned to Service - after Found

Date Returned to Service [   ]

Property Rec'd By [   ]

Disposition Approved By [   ]

If Auction - Batch No [   ]

Bill of Sale / Gain (Loss) Record

Remove Property Tag After Payment   ○ Sold Directly   ○ Sale by Auctioneer/Sales Agency

Date Sold [   ] Buyer [   ] Bill of Sale No [   ] Sale Amt [$500.00]

Book Value [$1,200.00]

Auctioneer or Consignee [   ] Reserve Amt [   ]

Salvage Value [$2,000.00]

Insured? ● Yes ○ No   Claim Proceeds [$10,000.00]

Requires contract under bailment & list by Batch No.of all assets consigned for sale

Gain or (Loss) [$7,300.00]

Sale Comments - include license requirements & permit numbers if required

[   ]

Seller:

Logo & Corporate Name
Contact Info

RECEIPT NO **000001**

BILL OF SALE
A Property Reserve Record

Date of Sale | 10/07/19

Buyer:

Name - individual or auction company | UBI No. | Phone
ABC | 000-000-000 | (425) 555-1000

Street Address | Email
1111 Main St. | buyer@abc.com | E-Mail PDF

City | State | Zip Code
Kirkland | WA | 98033

List of Items Purchased

Item	Make	MN	SN	Description	Price Each
1	HP	X100	1234567865432	PC Tower	$1,500.00

| 1 | Table scrolls and prints to (# of pages) |

Total Net Amount	$1,500.00
Shipping + Handling	
Sales Tax	
Credit	
Amount PAID	$1,500.00

Credit Card - required for individuals

Last 4 Digits

Buyer's Ck No

Buyer's Bank Account No

Terms of Sale:

Buyer hereby agrees that all sales are final and "AS IS". Seller offers no warranty nor is Seller liable in any way for any damages or injuries as result of the use of the sale items listed above.

Buyer's Signature | 10/07/19

John Hancock

Thank you for your business.
Check our website for additional sales or auctions of used equipment.

Use Topaz Signature Pad

FORM No./ Rev. 08-03-023-A

Void Transaction | Export

Consignor
Logo & Corporate Name
Contact Info

CONSIGNMENT RECORD
A Property Reserve Record

Consignee:

Date 10/06/19

Auction Company or Consignee Name	UBI No.	Phone
ABC	000-000-000	(425) 555-1000 x25

Street Address	Email	
1111 Main St	xxx@auctionco.com	E-Mail PDF

City	State	Zip Code
Kirkland	WA	98033

List of Items Consigned:

Item	Property No	Make	Description	MN	SN	Reserve Amt
1	E-01-00001	HP	PC Tower	X100	123456789	$1,500.00

1	Total Items	Table scrolls and prints to (# of pages)	Total Amt Based on Reserves	$1,500.00

Terms of Consignment:

Consignee hereby agrees that all items listed above are under bailment and if not sold within the deadline below, all unsold items will be returned within (10) days thereof. No items shall be sold below the set reserve amount above or scraped unless expressed permission in writing is granted by consignor. Upon completion of auction or sale, within (30) days, consignee shall deliver to consignor proof of payment received for each item sold along with payment in USD for all consigned items sold. Consignee shall make clear to it's customers that no warranty extends to them and shall remove all Consignor's Property labels upon sale. Both parties undersigned below agree to these terms.

Auction and/or sale shall be completed by

Consignee's Authorized Signature   Consignment Approved By

Use Topaz Signature Pad

Fee Paid   Net Proceeds   Ck No

FORM No./ Rev.

113

Page 1 of 1

Logo & Company Name
Address
Contact Information

Course No **0001**

COURSE CURRICULUM

Release Date

Rev A

Ref Plan No

Ref Top Assy No

Ref Task Assy No

Task Description

Min. Qual

Click Icon to View Video

YouTube Security Options:
1. Password Entry
2. Private posting
3. Public posting
Use level (2) unless otherwise instructed. Proprietary related instructions are linked to the LAN server.

https://www.youtube-nocookie.com/embed/E9rFYe519zQ?rel=0
Please wait a few seconds for video to load

Instructions: Include any information regarding safety issues related to the work area environment as well as any protective attire that may be required for the task. Issue any prints or process control documents, attire, and tools related to the task as well as kit parts necessary for the trainee to better understand the process involved. Interview the trainee both before to cover all benchmarks for performance standards and immediately after any sample lots are made to inspect and gauge competence.

Curriculum

APPENDIX W Part 1

Entry Qualification Codes:
A = BS/MS Degree
B = AA Degree
C = Vocational Training
D = Certification
E = HS/GED

Signature

Form No 04-02-001-A

Curriculum - continued

Page Test

Tips on Video Production:
Use the Windows* Snipping tool or some other screen capture program to capture the opening the closing frame for insertion at the front and back of your video production. There are any number of video editing software programs. We used VideoPad* by NCH. If a Screen recorder is required to record mouse movements on the screen for instructional purposes we employ ZD Soft*.   For editing .jpg stills we use Infanview*. For a camcoder we employ a Canon PowerShot* and for Audio Dubbing we use a Philips Voice Tracer* 2000 and MS Word to draft scripts in advance. Change the You Tube URL using the prefix (**https://www.youtube-nocookie.com/embed/**) and suffix (**?rel=0**) to allow the viewer to see only your video.

Aspect Ratio = 16:9 (1280 x 720) YouTube Standard   File Type: .mpg

INTRODUCING

Course No	Rev
0001	A

Course Description

Logo & Company Name
Contact Information

THE END

Course No	Rev
0001	A

Contact your supervisor for further instructions

© Copyright 20## Your Company Name
All Rights Reserved

www.yourdomain.com
name@yourdomain.com

Logo & Company Name
Contact Information

Logo & Company Name
Address
Contact Information

INTERNAL AUDIT REPORT

Report Date: 02/17/20

This eform was designed to record the results of an internal audit of the following data collection recordsets and financial journals and ledgers for each reporting period. Pages 3-7 are listings of data collection records and the range of record numbers for each finance reporting period. Upon completion of each batch recordset review, a report should be generated using the specified Excel SaveAs file. The appointed auditor should have access to all eform recordsets listed before in order to verify they have been processed according to the identified process control directive. Search is via QMS subpart directive and eform number listed below - accessed from the server. Policy references listed in each subpart directive. Static data is set to memorize from eform record to record to speed audit manhours.

PROCUREMENT

Form No	Rev.	Task Directive	Audit Directive	Audited
				☐ Department Requisitions
				☐ VQS - Vendor Qualification Surveys
				☐ Vendor Profile & Periodic Status Records
				☐ RFQ - Requests for Quotation
				☐ Bid Form Records
				☐ Purchase Orders
				☐ Daily Rec'g Log - for reporting period
				☐ Discrepancy Records
				☐ AP Vouchers
				☐ AP Checklist Records

ASSET RECORDING & TRACKING

Form No	Rev.	Task Directive	Audit Directive	Audited
				☐ Property Records
				☐ Cost Basis Records
				☐ Tool Crib & Storage Site Records
				☐ Asset Tracker Records

○ Yes ○ No
Do All Property Records include placement date, map location, make, model, serial number, cost basis, and classification plus other field data for traceability, do they match asset tags, and are they current?

○ Yes ○ No Are Asset Tracking Devices & Software in Good Working Order?

○ Yes ○ No Adequate Inventory of Tracking Labels and/or RFID Tags?

○ Yes ○ No Are all assets properly tagged with barcoded label and/or RFID tags?

○ Yes ○ No Have missing or end-of-life assets been purged from listings of in-use assets?

FORM No. 05-04-006-A

Logo & Company Name
Address
Contact Information

Control No.　000001

Report Date:　02/17/20

DISPOSITION

Form No	Rev.	Task Directive	Audit Directive	Audited
				☐ Asset Disposition Report

Form No	Rev.	Task Directive	Audit Directive	Audited
				☐ Batch Consignments

Form No	Rev.	Task Directive	Audit Directive	Audited
				☐ Bills of Sale

Number of assets that reached their End-of-Life this fiscal period? ____

Number of assets that have gone missing this fiscal period? ____　Value at Cost Basis ____

◯ Yes ◯ No　Have all these assets been removed from their designated map locations and put in a locked quarantined area?

◯ Yes ◯ No　Have all End-of-Life and Missing assets been removed from the master listings for capitalized assets?

◯ Yes ◯ No　Have all End-of-Life and Missing assets been removed from the master listings for expensed assets?

Number of assets flagged for PM this fiscal period? ____

◯ Yes ◯ No　Was PM completed for all assets tagged for PM? If No, how many are pending PM? ____

Number of assets donated this fiscal period? ____　Value at Cost Basis? ____

Number of assets sold by contract Auctioneer? ____　Value at Cost Basis? ____

Number of assets sold directly out of property reserve? ____　Value at Cost Basis? ____

◯ Yes ◯ No　Does Gain or Loss match reports and GL Accounts?

FINANCIAL OPERATIONS

◯ Yes ◯ No　Disbursement Journal reconciled to Check Register?

◯ Yes ◯ No　Cash Receipts & Sales Journal reconciled with Check Register Deposits?

◯ Yes ◯ No　Do the two reconciled journals above match GL accounts?

◯ Yes ◯ No　Adequate notes to financials for all adjustments, additions, and deletions to GL ?

PROCESS DIRECTIVES

◯ Yes ◯ No　Are Volume II QMS Directives current?

How many revisions in this period? ____　◯ Yes ◯ No　Were they all validated for efficacy?

TRAINING DIRECTIVES

◯ Yes ◯ No　Are all training Directives, Qualification, and Certification requirements current?

How many certifications issued this fiscal period? ____

◯ Yes ◯ No　Are all company & department org charts and corresponding Job Descriptions current?

Reviewed by		Audit by	
Name & Title		Name & Title	

PROCUREMENT RECORDS

Report Period - FYE:

Line	Form No	Rev	Record Title	Seed Record No.	Ending Record No	Audit Completed Date & Time
1	08-01-001	A	Department Requisitions	00001	00005	2/17/2020 3:24:26 PM
2	08-01-002	A	Vendor Qualification Surveys	00001	00003	
3	08-01-003	A	Vendor Profiles	00001	00003	
4	08-01-004	A	RFQ	00001	00005	
5	08-01-005	A	Bid Forms	00001	00002	
6	08-01-006	A	PO	00001	00005	
7	08-01-007	A	Daily Receiving Log	00001	00001	
8	08-01-008	A	Discrepancy Record	00001	00001	
9	05-01-009	A	AP Voucher	00001	00005	
10	05-01-010	A	AP Checklist Record	00001	00003	

10 Total Recordsets for this Process

Table above scrolls and prints to additional pages

ASSETS & TRACKING RECORDS

Line	Form No	Rev	Record Title	Seed Record No.	Ending Record No	Audit Completed Date & Time
1	08-02-001		Property Records	00001	00002	2/17/2020 6:47:45 PM
2	08-02-002		Cost Basis Records	00001		
3	08-02-003		Tool Crib Records	00001		
4	08-02-004		Asset Tracker Records	00001		
5	08-02-00X		Dept Storage Cabinet Records	00001		

5 Total Recordsets for this Process

Table above scrolls and prints to additional pages

DISPOSITION RECORDS

Line	Form No	Rev	Record Title	Seed Record No.	Ending Record No	Audit Completed Date & Time
1	08-03-001	A	Disposition Records	00001		
2	08-03-002	A	Batch Consignments	00001		
3	08-03-003	A	Property Reserve Bills of Sale	00001		

3 Total Recordsets for this Process

Table above scrolls and prints to additional pages

Audit by

I Attest that I carefully reviewed all the records in each recordset listed above and found them to be property completed and locked with certificate-based signatures that match the processing date.

Name & Title

ECM (Enterprise Content Management) Schema

NOTE:
Whatever file and storage convention you adopt for your business it should accommodate all operating files. We used a two digit prefix assigned to each department as displayed below in the Org Chart. Additional prefix digits can also be used for 2nd line staff to maintain control over your entire operations.

Data folders should include pictures, video, sound, or whatever other source files required for your business or apps it may use. Files may also be broken down by project, products, or services. Passwords should be cataloged for each user authorized to access data records and a current list should be maintained by IT. Templates should only be accessed and issued by IT or top management. How you grant access and what level of authorization is permitted should be documented as a matter of policy. This should be designed per your OMS (Quality Management System).

Each department will have its own specific file sets. While searching for files users should be able to open a directive that includes a convention for naming and retrieving any file via its assigned coded filename using an updated index. ADHOC files are named and stored by subject by date and in alphabetical order.

Pyramid Organizational Chart

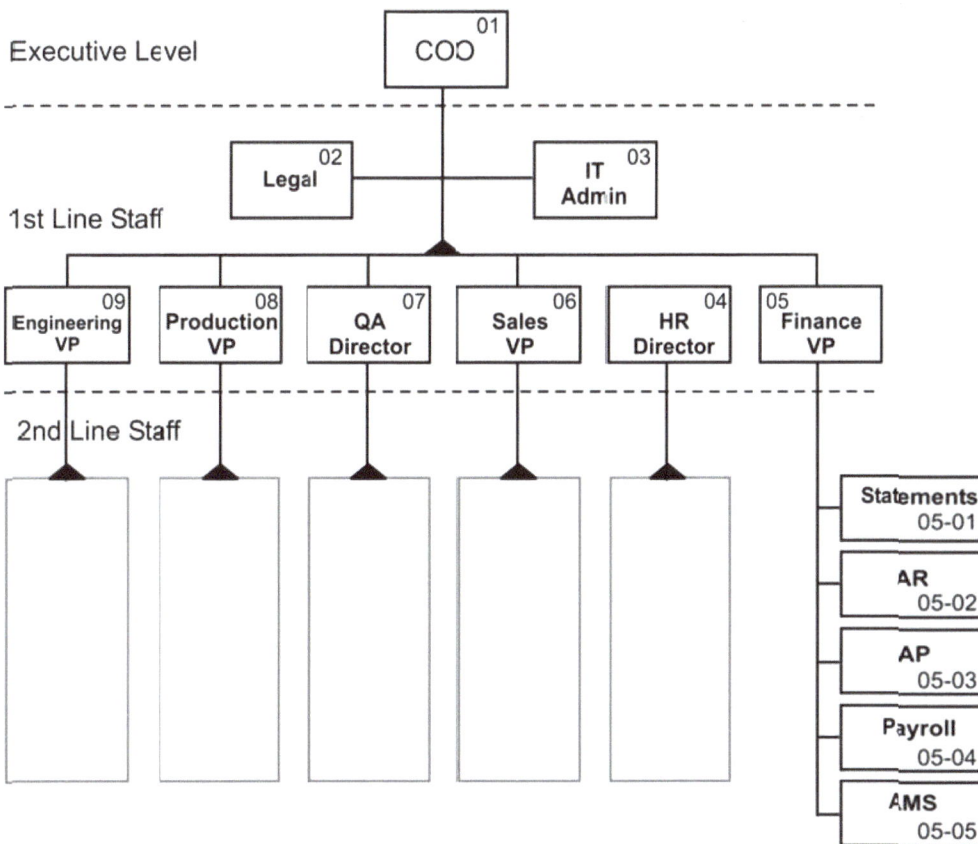

Additional Hierarchical Staff Levels to Factory Floor

The file tree structure (right column):

- DATA
  - FORMS
    - 01-Admin
    - 02-Legal
    - 03-DCR Mgmt
    - 04-HR Mgmt
    - 04-HR Training
    - 05-AP
    - 05-AR
    - 05-Assets
      - 08-Directives
      - AD-Hoc Files
      - Archives
      - eForms
      - Excel Files
        - Masters
        - Reports
      - PDF Files
        - Masters
        - Reports
    - 05-Finance
    - 05-Payroll
    - 06-Sales
    - 07-QA Complaints
    - 07-QA QMS
    - 07-Regulatory
    - 08-Inventory
    - 08-Mfg Operations

Basic Network Schema for IT Control Over Data Collection Documents

Note: Formdocs* eForms protocols
Upon loading the software a sample set of eForm templates is automatically loaded under your Application Data folder or Program Application Data folder depending on your OS using the following directory paths:

For Windows XP
C:/Documents and Settings/All Users/Application Data/Formdocs/Templates/(Dept Sub Folders) filename. Fdt
Formdocs version 9.6 will run on Windows XP

For Windows 7 or 10
C:/Program Data/Formdocs/Templates/(Dept Sub Folders) filename. Fdt
Formdocs version 10.X will only run on Windows 7, 8, or 10

TIP: To keep the main Templates folder for operations uncluttered we recommend you move the Templates files that came with the program into a folder named Samples. All Template files have a *.Fdt extension and eForm recordset files use a *.Fdd extension that can be stored in your LAN server or Cloud account. We also recommend that you keep the *.Fdn serial number files and the *.Fdi (index) files with the *.Fdd files in each Subfolder. To eliminate any confusion we use the same subfolder names and file names for both our and *.Fdt Template and *.Fdd recordset files. We use shortcuts on each User's work station to open batch recordset files needed for view or process.

Any revisions to the *.Fdt Templates should be recorded in your DCR system. An eForm should be designed for that purpose. An archive should be configured for inactive Templates or batch recordsets should be cataloged for reference when revised or replaced with a new batch, respectively.

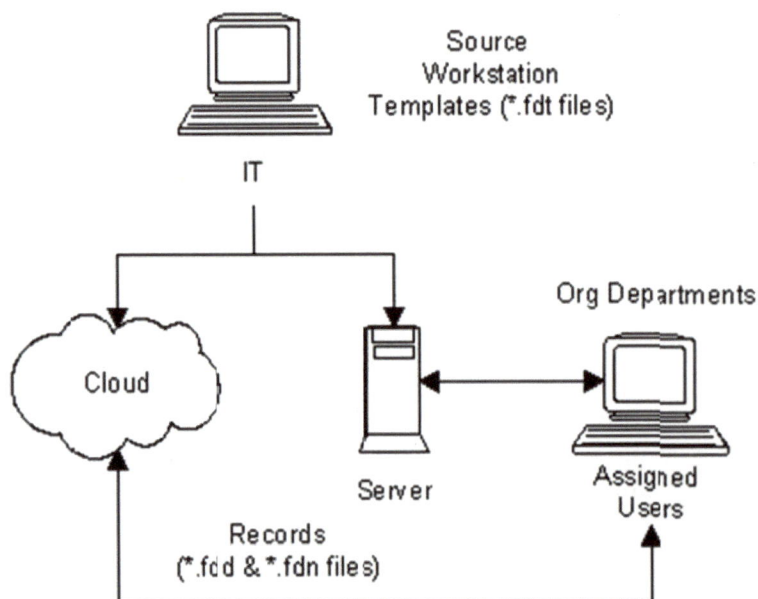

Refer to Figure 4.2 in chapter (4) for a more detailed Network System Architecture.